Copyright

The Manifesting Playbook by Coach Brandon Ward Sr.

Published by Aplaceforyourvision.com _as Vegas, NV 89108

www.iambrandonward.us

© 2020 Brandon Ward

CopyrightDepot.com number 00069634-1

All rights reserved. No portion of this book may be reproduced in any form without permission from the publisher, except as permitted by U.S. copyright law. For permissions contact:

brandonward@dreamsafe.org

Paper Back ISBN: 978-1-7350486-9-7

Introduction

The intent of this book is to set the reader on the path of accomplishing his ultimate goals and handling the everyday responsibilities of being a man, husband, father, provider, leader, and master of himself. As a certified Life Coach, Business Coach, Business Owner, Non-Profit Founder, and Motivational Speaker, I Brandon Ward have dedicated my life to improving the lives of others through Personal and Business Development. I am a firm believer in leadership, mentorship, and coaching no matter a person's level of achievement. The best of the best in the world all have coaches, some even have two or three for different areas of their lives. Not all can afford coaching, nor do all need one to accomplish their goals. Some just need self-discipline, accountability, a plan, and the drive to overcome every obstacle before them. I have created this Play Book as a guide to align you with your purpose and capture the "receipts" as you dominate this quarter, month by month, week by week, and day by day. As you PURPOSEFULLY move closer to your destiny.

In this book you will identify who you are through affirmations. Self-evaluate what you have acquired. Identify Strengths, Weaknesses, and Aspirations. Your learning and way of thinking (DISC). Your Goals (Long, medium, and short term). Your VISION, MISSION, and PURPOSE. Friendship and the Law of Attraction. Available resources that you are or are not taking advantage of to leverage your life. "Life Anchors," what is slowing you down or holding you back. The formula and strategy for change. The power of intention, clarity, and taking ACTION.

This playbook is a 90 day plan to guide you closer to your success. Keeping you true to yourself and your mission. Life is offensive and defensive. With the right player (you), the right system (this playbook), and me as your coach, we will not lose.

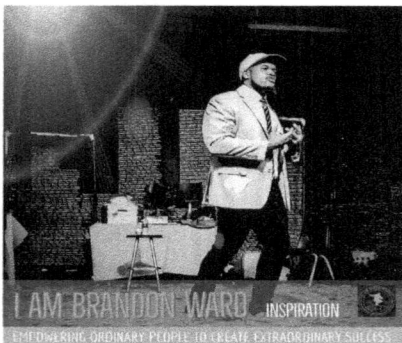

I AM BRANDON WARD INSPIRATION
EMPOWERING ORDINARY PEOPLE TO CREATE EXTRAORDINARY SUCCESS

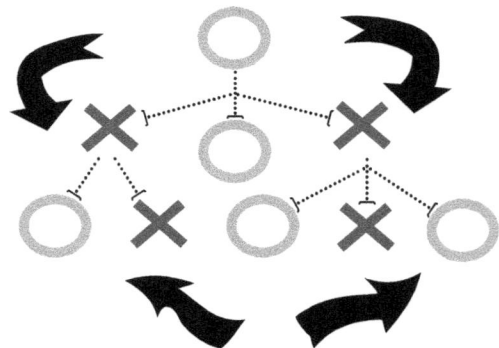

Who I AM

Look around, In the current times culture has completely created a massive number of followers and not enough leaders. The power of information and marketing itself specifically targets certain types of people, pushing their agenda and thoughts leaving people misinformed, distracted, and choosing a side. This mindset alone will have a person acting outside of themselves in order to fit in. It is important that we personally identify ourselves, who we are, and what we stand for. This is done by recording your affirmations, also known as "I AM Statements." Such as I AM becoming my greatest self. I AM a leader. I AM healthy, ect... These statements should be read daily or whenever you feel self-doubt or self-sabotage.

Below fill in the blanks with your personal I AM Statements.

I AM _____

I AM _____

I AM _____

I AM _____

I AM _____

I AM _____

I AM _____

I AM _____

I AM _____

I AM _____

I AM _____

I AM _____

I AM _____

I AM _____

I AM _____

I AM _____

I AM _____

Evaluate

In order to start any journey, you must first do an inspection of the current conditions. We have been many places and experienced many things. As we move forward, we will utilize the skills and knowledge acquired, but first let's evaluate the vessel. Time for a checkup. Health may be most important. Schedule a check up with your doctor or neighborhood Pharmacy. The results from the check up will set you pace for this journey moving ahead. What is your weight, credit score, happiness level, resume, awards, achievements, and accolades.?

_____

_____

_____

_____

_____

_____

_____

_____

_____

_____

_____

_____

_____

_____

_____

_____

_____

_____

_____

Strengths, Weaknesses, Aspirations

If you have ever wondered when it was necessary to use your EGO, this would be the perfect time. Identify your strengths. Write down all the gifts that God has blessed you with and those you have developed. Also, identify your weaknesses and areas for improvement. Lastly, identify your aspirations. You know what your capable of, especially with a coach behind you.

I am gifted and talented at:

1. _____
2. _____
3. _____
4. _____
5. _____

My areas of weakness are:

1. _____
2. _____
3. _____
4. _____
5. _____

My aspirations are:

1. _____
2. _____
3. _____
4. _____
5. _____

I am capable of:

1. _____
2. _____
3. _____
4. _____
5. _____

Left Brain, Right Brain

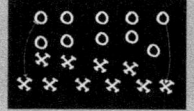

LEFT

LOGIC
ANALYSIS
SEQUENCING
LINEAR
MATHEMATICS
LANGUAGE
FACTS
THINK IN WORDS
LYRICS
COMPUTATION

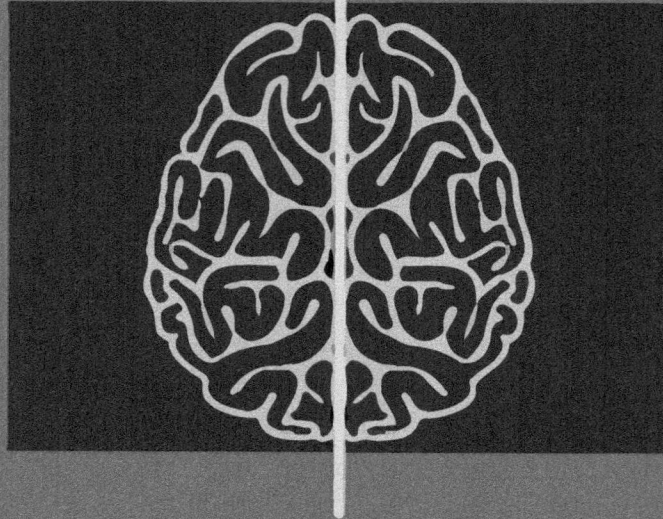

RIGHT

CREATIVITY
IMAGINATION
SPIRITUAL
INTUITION
ARTS
RHYTHM
(Beats)
NON-VERBAL
FEELINGS/EMPATHY
VISUALIZATION

Why is it important that both the left and right hemispheres work in harmony? It's because they both contribute to a brain's capacity for thinking. The two hemispheres of the brain connect to the corpus callosum.

The cerebrum is the main part of the brain that deals with thinking. It helps with learning and language and assists with body movements such as walking and dancing.

You gotta love the person you are becoming. If not, it is time to make some hard changes. Every day we must heal and get better.

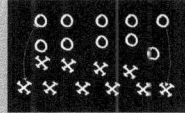

Learning takes time, money, and sacrifice. How you spend your time and what you spend your time learning will greatly impact your life positively or negatively. Addicted 2 Success has identified these nine skills as skills that need to be developed in order to be successful. How can you develop the following skills? What books can you read? What course can you take? What group can you join? What specialist can you see?

1. Communication ☐
2. Presentation Skills ☐
3. Reasoning ☐
4. Technical Literacy ☐
5. Analytical ☐
6. Leadership ☐
7. Flexibility ☐
8. Interpersonal ☐
9. Anger Management ☐

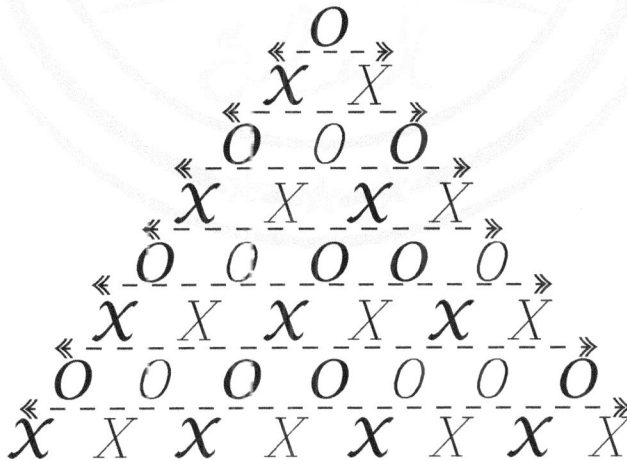

Big dreams with limited vision. A great Coach will help you map out the plan, but first let's overcome what's holding you back.

Layers of Comfort

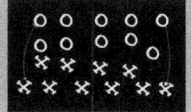

The comfort zone is a safe space where we do not risk, but neither do we grow. It is not simply a physical space but a mental concept. It is not limited to a secure cord we have built around us but includes both our daily routines and way of thinking. Therefore, it can become the perfect excuse not to do, not to risk, not to grow, and ultimately not live.

Magical things happen outside the comfort zone, change and growth occur, but there is also the dreaded panic zone, so it's important to find a right balance in life based on a deep knowledge of what is comfort zone and what we can find when we overcome its limits.

LAYERS OF COMFORT

Description	Zone
Feels safe and in control. No growth.	COMFORT ZONE
Anxious, stress, and doubt.	PANIC ZONE
Lack of self confidence. Finds excuses. Is affected by other's opinions.	FEAR ZONE
Deals with challenges and problems. Acquires new skills. Extend your comfort zone.	LEARNING ZONE
Find purpose and live dreams. Set new goals. Conquer objectives.	GROWTH ZONE

One of the best parts of this journey is the people you meet with the same passion as you. These people are special, because God has a way of sending you support exactly when we need it.

Goals

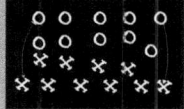

Goals make life worth living. I went a couple of years in this lifetime where I set no goals for myself, and those years I accomplished nothing and went nowhere. Experiencing tragedy and pain will do that to you, and the process of healing will leave you stagnant. Many of my family members have lost their way do to not setting goals. You will get lost in this world not knowing where you are headed. Goals are like GPS to our future setting the correct path ahead for us to follow. Below write your 5 Year goals, 3 year goals, and 1 year goal. We will break this down later.

5 Year Goals

_____
_____
_____
_____
_____
_____
_____

3 Year Goals

_____
_____
_____
_____
_____
_____
_____

1 Year Goals

_____
_____
_____
_____
_____
_____
_____

Vision, Mission, Purpose

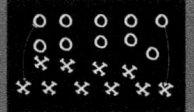

Your Vision

Your vision statement reveals the highest level you plan to achieve in the long term to reach personal fulfillment. This is your Legacy, what you stand for, and what you will pass down once your gone. This is how you will be remembered and how you will leave your mark on The World.

Everyday, my Legacy awakes me, I am creating my Legacy.

My Vision

_____

_____

Your Mission

Your mission is the steps and activity needed in order to achieve your vision. What resources are needed? What qualification? Who do you need to know? What do you need to achieve or acquire? What must you learn and what must get done?

My Mission

_____

_____

Your Purpose

Your purpose is whatever God, or the Universe has given you as your responsibilities. What must you do, or the world or people will suffer? Children, family, skill, gifts.

My Purpose

_____

_____

Purpose

_____

_____

Purpose

_____

_____

Core Values List

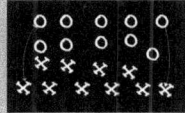

* Authenticity
* Achievement
* Adventure
* Authority
* Autonomy
* Balance
* Beauty
* Boldness
* Compassion
* Challenge
* Citizenship
* Community
* Competency
* Contribution
* Creativity
* Curiosity
* Determination
* Fairness
* Faith
* Fame
* Friendships
* Fun
* Growth
* Happiness
* Honesty
* Humor
* Influence
* Inner Harmony
* Justice

* Kindness
* Knowledge
* Leadership
* Learning
* Love
* Loyalty
* Meaningful Work
* Openness
* Optimism
* Peace
* Pleasure
* Poise
* Popularity
* Recognition
* Religion
* Reputation
* Respect
* Responsibility
* Security
* Self-Respect
* Service
* Spirituality
* Stability
* Success
* Status,
* Trustworthiness
* Wealth
* Wisdom

Core Values

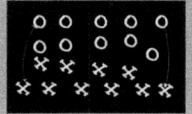

What values do you need to have in order to become who you are becoming and get to where you are headed. List the words from the previous page. Feel free to add any if you do not see it there..

1. _____
2. _____
3. _____
4. _____
5. _____
6. _____
7. _____
8. _____
9. _____
10. _____
11. _____
12. _____
13. _____
14. _____
15. _____

There is a road created for your destiny. You just need to find it.

Energy

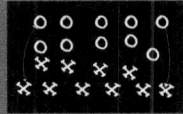

Everything in life is energy, who you are and the actions you take decide the level of force behind it. As source energy, we attract other energy and are susceptible to their influences. Whether negative or positive, one has energy that can be completely shifted by another. Some energy drains you and some energy empowers you.

Take inventory of the energy around you, and the energy of the environments you put yourself in. Then take inventory of the people around you. Are they charging or draining you? Observe your activities and your level of participation. Is it draining you or driving you? Lastly, is your effort and energy helping or helping the team, family, group, or friendship?

Key players in my life:

Name:	Name:
Relationship: Known for how long:	Relationship: Known for how long:
How they make me feel:	How they make me feel:
Together we can:	Together we can:
Last time contacted, contact #, contact emai	Last time contacted, contact #, contact email
How I can help them:	How I can help them:
How they can help me:	How they can help me:

Name:	Name:
Relationship: Known for how long:	Relationship: Known for how long:
How they make me feel:	How they make me feel:
Together we can:	Together we can:
Last time contacted, contact #, contact ema l	Last time contacted, contact #, contact email
How I can help them:	How I can help them:
How they can help me:	How they can help me:

Resources

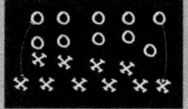

In the game of life everything around you and everyone you know is a resource. You do not need the entirety of the person, just the resource they hold for you. As human beings we are all connected some way or form. I truly believe that God, the Universe, Higher Power, ect, perfectly orchestrates our entire journey in order to move closer to our destiny.

Below identify the resources around you. Are you taking advantage of those resources? Why not, how, and when should you take action?

Identify resources that you need; people to meet, supplies, money, credit, transportation, skill. You'll find everything that you need is within reach or already provided.

_____
_____
_____
_____
_____
_____
_____
_____
_____
_____
_____
_____
_____
_____
_____
_____
_____
_____

Life Anchors

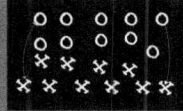

I have picked up and dropped many things in my life. Letting go of what no longer serves me, but sometimes holding on too long and experiencing the damages.

What is stopping you or slowing you down on this journey? What and who is no longer serving you? What beliefs are holding you back mentally? What do you fear that is limiting you? What skill can you develop? What habits are suppressing you? When will you let go and stop sacrificing yourself?

Habits

Affects

Plan

Habits

Affects

Plan

Habits

Affects

Plan

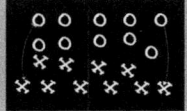

Change

Dannemiller Formula for Change: C = D × V × F > R

(C)hange occurs when (D)issatisfaction x (V)ision x (F)irst Steps is "greater" than the (R)esistance

Dissatisfaction is a strong encourager of change, when you feel it begin to act on your vision. Make sure you have one; your vision was written earlier on page 9. Now you must know what steps need to be taken and take the first step. Getting the momentum going will help to overcome all resistance.

Clarity x Action = Success

Be clear, study, learn, then take action.

Intention

Merriam-Webster dictionary describes Intention as having the mind, attention, or will concentrated on something or some end or purpose.

I say the energy and action put behind something to create a specific result. Intentions and be good and evil. Be aware of the outcome of your thought and actions. What you intend will result.

Effort

Merriam-Webster dictionary describes effort as a: conscious exertion of power: hard work

I say your effort is how much you care or are willing to sacrifice in order to accomplish this mission. It is not a comfortable ride, it will definitely get bumpy. This mission is one of emotion and heartache, but at the finish line it will all be worth it. The passion is in the journey.

Are you making a change?

What is your intention?

What will be your level of effort?

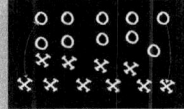

Dear Reader,

As you embark on your journey, I am pleased to be a part of the process. I created this 90-day journal to set you on your path and hold you accountable daily, as you take the steps necessary to make continued progress. This is the same journal that I use myself in keeping up with the many activities that I am a part of. I wasn't introduced to this method until the age of 35. No one had ever taught me the strategies of planning and accomplishing goals. For many years I just wrote down to do like grocery list and checked off the items. There have been many appointments that I have missed or was late for, do to my poor planning practices. As I became a business owner and Co-Founder of DreamSAFE Project with my wife Tiffany Ward, it was a must that I learned new strategies, and implement them. I now rarely waste time and get stuff done daily. Many of us get caught up staying active and busy, but not accomplishing anything. In today's world the people want consistency. Your children, your spouse, your boss, your employees, your followers, and you yourself.

They say don't worry about what you can't control. One thing we must be in control of is our time. With control of time comes control of life. In memory of the late Nipsey Hussel "The Marathon Continues."
LETS GO!

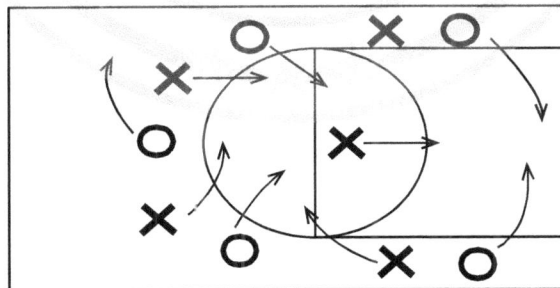

First you tame the beast, then you train the beast. Discover its strengths and its passions and apply it to a purpose.

PlayBook Calender

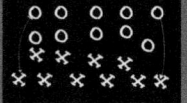

Month:_____   Year:_____

Monday	Tuesday	Wednesday	Thursday	Friday	Saturday	Sunday

Events	Important Dates	Social Events	Meetings

Weekly Playbook Focus Sheet

Name:_____

Weekending:_____   Date:_____ /_____ /_____

*The Number 1 Thing I Must Achieve This Week: _____

*Goals & Actions before next week:	Goal Achieved?	Comments:
Goal 1	☐ Yes ☐ No	
Goal 2	☐ Yes ☐ No	
Goal 3	☐ Yes ☐ No	
Goal 4	☐ Yes ☐ No	

My brightest achievement in the week just past:

My main challenge during the week gone:

Something that I learned through reading, listening to a tape, watching a video or living life:

At the moment, my greatest focus in life is:

I can find help by :

Briefly speaking :	I've concentrated on:	I've also worked on:
☐ I spent _____ hrs. working ON myself this last week	☐ Health	☐ Relationships
☐ My motivation level is at _____ %	☐ Education	☐ Communication
☐ Life is _____	☐ Income	☐ Planning
	☐ Love	☐ Leadership
	☐ Spirituality	☐ Best Effort

Daily Play Book.

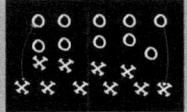

Time	Activity	Outcome / Notes
06:00		
06:30		
07:00		
07:30		
08:00		
08:30		
09:00		
09:30		
10:00		
10:30		
11:00		
11:30		
12:00		
12:30		
13:00		
13:30		
14:00		
14:30		
15:00		
15:30		
16:00		
16:30		
17:00		
17:30		
18:00		
18:30		
19:00		
19:30		
20:00		
20:30		
21:00		

Date:

Daily I AMs

I AM

I AM

I AM

I AM

I AM

Tasks I have to do today which contribute to my quarter goals

1.
2.
3.
4.
5.
6.

PRIORITY FOLLOW UP CALL/EMAIL

1.
2.
3.
4.
5.
6.

OTHER TASKS / OR TO DELEGATE

1.
2.
3.
4.
5.

Sacrifice who you are, for the person you will become.

Daily Play Book.

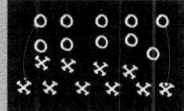

Date:

Time	Activity	Outcome / Notes
06:00		
06:30		
07:00		
07:30		
08:00		
08:30		
09:00		
09:30		
10:00		
10:30		
11:00		
11:30		
12:00		
12:30		
13:00		
13:30		
14:00		
14:30		
15:00		
15:30		
16:00		
16:30		
17:00		
17:30		
18:00		
18:30		
19:00		
19:30		
20:00		
20:30		
21:00		

Daily I AMs

I AM

I AM

I AM

I AM

I AM

Tasks I have to do today which contribute to my quarter goals

1.
2.
3.
4.
5.
6.

PRIORITY FOLLOW UP CALL/EMAIL

1.
2.
3.
4.
5.
6.

OTHER TASKS / OR TO DELEGATE

1.
2.
3.
4.
5.

If an opportunity exists, I will be there. For I know there is something that exist, for me to advance in my next level of development.

Daily Play Book.

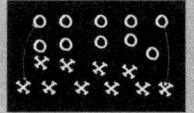

Time	Activity	Outcome / Notes
06:00		
06:30		
07:00		
07:30		
08:00		
08:30		
09:00		
09:30		
10:00		
10:30		
11:00		
11:30		
12:00		
12:30		
13:00		
13:30		
14:00		
14:30		
15:00		
15:30		
16:00		
16:30		
17:00		
17:30		
18:00		
18:30		
19:00		
19:30		
20:00		
20:30		
21:00		

Date:

Daily I AMs

I AM

I AM

I AM

I AM

I AM

Tasks I have to do today which contribute to my quarter goals

1.
2.
3.
4.
5.
6.

PRIORITY FOLLOW UP CALL/EMAIL

1.
2.
3.
4.
5.
6.

OTHER TASKS / OR TO DELEGATE

1.
2.
3.
4.
5.

Working with a coach is going to take you out of your comfort zone, you must be ready for change.

Daily Play Book.

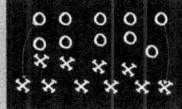

Time	Activity	Outcome / Notes
06:00		
06:30		
07:00		
07:30		
08:00		
08:30		
09:00		
09:30		
10:00		
10:30		
11:00		
11:30		
12:00		
12:30		
13:00		
13:30		
14:00		
14:30		
15:00		
15:30		
16:00		
16:30		
17:00		
17:30		
18:00		
18:30		
19:00		
19:30		
20:00		
20:30		
21:00		

Daily I AMs

I AM

I AM

I AM

I AM

I AM

Tasks I have to do today which contribute to my quarter goals

1.
2.
3.
4.
5.
6.

PRIORITY FOLLOW UP CALL/EMAIL

1.
2.
3.
4.
5.
6.

OTHER TASKS / OR TO DELEGATE

1.
2.
3.
4.
5.

Once man can distinguish between an opportunity and a test, he eliminates a future of negative events, and strengthens his ability to achieve his destiny.

Daily Play Book.

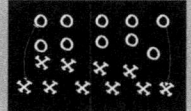

Time	Activity	Outcome / Notes
06:00		
06:30		
07:00		
07:30		
08:00		
08:30		
09:00		
09:30		
10:00		
10:30		
11:00		
11:30		
12:00		
12:30		
13:00		
13:30		
14:00		
14:30		
15:00		
15:30		
16:00		
16:30		
17:00		
17:30		
18:00		
18:30		
19:00		
19:30		
20:00		
20:30		
21:00		

Date:

Daily I AMs

I AM

I AM

I AM

I AM

I AM

Tasks I have to do today which contribute to my quarter goals

1.
2.
3.
4.
5.
6.

PRIORITY FOLLOW UP CALL/EMAIL

1.
2.
3.
4.
5.
6.

OTHER TASKS / OR TO DELEGATE

1.
2.
3.
4.
5.

As a child I always wanted to be a Superhero. I finally found my Power.

Daily Play Book.

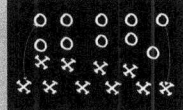

Time	Activity	Outcome / Notes
06:00		
06:30		
07:00		
07:30		
08:00		
08:30		
09:00		
09:30		
10:00		
10:30		
11:00		
11:30		
12:00		
12:30		
13:00		
13:30		
14:00		
14:30		
15:00		
15:30		
16:00		
16:30		
17:00		
17:30		
18:00		
18:30		
19:00		
19:30		
20:00		
20:30		
21:00		

Date:

Daily I AMs

I AM
I AM
I AM
I AM
I AM

Tasks I have to do today which contribute to my quarter goals

1.
2.
3.
4.
5.
6.

PRIORITY FOLLOW UP CALL/EMAIL

1.
2.
3.
4.
5.
6.

OTHER TASKS / OR TO DELEGATE

1.
2.
3.
4.
5.

I am up because I am trying to catch up. A whole village is depending on my success.

Daily Play Book.

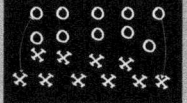

Time	Activity	Outcome / Notes
06:00		
06:30		
07:00		
07:30		
08:00		
08:30		
09:00		
09:30		
10:00		
10:30		
11:00		
11:30		
12:00		
12:30		
13:00		
13:30		
14:00		
14:30		
15:00		
15:30		
16:00		
16:30		
17:00		
17:30		
18:00		
18:30		
19:00		
19:30		
20:00		
20:30		
21:00		

Date:

Daily I AMs

I AM

I AM

I AM

I AM

I AM

Tasks I have to do today which contribute to my quarter goals

1.
2.
3.
4.
5.
6.

PRIORITY FOLLOW UP CALL/EMAIL

1.
2.
3.
4.
5.
6.

OTHER TASKS / OR TO DELEGATE

1.
2.
3.
4.
5.

We do not need permission.

Weekly Summary

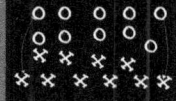

WEEKLY SUMMARY SCORING	Score 1 -10
My focus on TOP weekly priorities...	
My Self Management Time Discipline	
Level of Activity	
Time on Goals	
Self Development	
Health	

BEST PART OF THE WEEK/WHERE I WAS OUTSTANDING & HOW I CELEBRATED
•
•
•

TOP LEARNINGS THIS WEEK
•
•
•

TOP CHALLENGES
•
•
•

TOP FOCUS FOR NEXT WEEK
•
•
•

I AM GRATEFUL FOR
•
•
•

Weekly Playbook Focus Sheet

Name:_____

Weekending:_____   Date:_____ /_____ /_____

*The Number 1 Thing I Must Achieve This Week: _____

*Goals & Actions before next week:	Goal Achieved?	Comments:
Goal 1	☐Yes ☐No	
Goal 2	☐Yes ☐No	
Goal 3	☐Yes ☐No	
Goal 4	☐Yes ☐No	

My brightest achievement in the week just past:

My main challenge during the week gone:

Something that I learned through reading, listening to a tape, watching a video or living life:

At the moment, my greatest focus in life is:

I can find help by :

Briefly speaking :

☐ I spent _____ hrs. working ON myself this last week

☐ My motivation level is at _____ %

☐ Life is _____

I've concentrated on:

☐ Health
☐ Education
☐ Income
☐ Love
☐ Spirituality

I've also worked on:

☐ Relationships
☐ Communication
☐ Planning
☐ Leadership
☐ Best Effort

Daily Play Book.

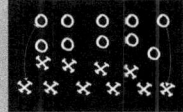

Time	Activity	Outcome / Notes
06:00		
06:30		
07:00		
07:30		
08:00		
08:30		
09:00		
09:30		
10:00		
10:30		
11:00		
11:30		
12:00		
12:30		
13:00		
13:30		
14:00		
14:30		
15:00		
15:30		
16:00		
16:30		
17:00		
17:30		
18:00		
18:30		
19:00		
19:30		
20:00		
20:30		
21:00		

Date:

Daily I AMs

I AM

I AM

I AM

I AM

I AM

Tasks I have to do today which contribute to my quarter goals

1.
2.
3.
4.
5.
6.

PRIORITY FOLLOW UP CALL/EMAIL

1.
2.
3.
4.
5.
6.

OTHER TASKS / OR TO DELEGATE

1.
2.
3.
4.
5.

I had to strip my mind of what I knew, so I could learn something new.

Daily Play Book.

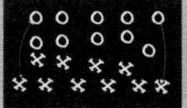

Date:

Time	Activity	Outcome / Notes
06:00		
06:30		
07:00		
07:30		
08:00		
08:30		
09:00		
09:30		
10:00		
10:30		
11:00		
11:30		
12:00		
12:30		
13:00		
13:30		
14:00		
14:30		
15:00		
15:30		
16:00		
16:30		
17:00		
17:30		
18:00		
18:30		
19:00		
19:30		
20:00		
20:30		
21:00		

Daily I AMs

I AM

I AM

I AM

I AM

I AM

Tasks I have to do today which contribute to my quarter goals

1.
2.
3.
4.
5.
6.

PRIORITY FOLLOW UP CALL/EMAIL

1.
2.
3.
4.
5.
6.

OTHER TASKS / OR TO DELEGATE

1.
2.
3.
4.
5.

Cherish those who feed you when the mind will not let you eat.

Daily Play Book.

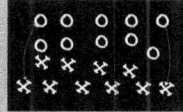

Date:

Time	Activity	Outcome / Notes
06:00		
06:30		
07:00		
07:30		
08:00		
08:30		
09:00		
09:30		
10:00		
10:30		
11:00		
11:30		
12:00		
12:30		
13:00		
13:30		
14:00		
14:30		
15:00		
15:30		
16:00		
16:30		
17:00		
17:30		
18:00		
18:30		
19:00		
19:30		
20:00		
20:30		
21:00		

Daily I AMs

I AM

I AM

I AM

I AM

I AM

Tasks I have to do today which contribute to my quarter goals

1.
2.
3.
4.
5.
6.

PRIORITY FOLLOW UP CALL/EMAIL

1.
2.
3.
4.
5.
6.

OTHER TASKS / OR TO DELEGATE

1.
2.
3.
4.
5.

No matter your faith. The most important person you can believe in is yourself.

Daily Play Book.

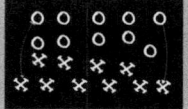

Date:

Time	Activity	Outcome / Notes
06:00		
06:30		
07:00		
07:30		
08:00		
08:30		
09:00		
09:30		
10:00		
10:30		
11:00		
11:30		
12:00		
12:30		
13:00		
13:30		
14:00		
14:30		
15:00		
15:30		
16:00		
16:30		
17:00		
17:30		
18:00		
18:30		
19:00		
19:30		
20:00		
20:30		
21:00		

Daily I AMs

I AM

I AM

I AM

I AM

I AM

Tasks I have to do today which contribute to my quarter goals

1.

2.

3.

4.

5.

6.

PRIORITY FOLLOW UP CALL/EMAIL

1.

2.

3.

4.

5.

6.

OTHER TASKS / OR TO DELEGATE

1.

2.

3.

4.

5.

All pain experienced made me stronger than ever before. Good days are upon us...

Daily Play Book.

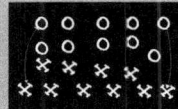

Date:

Time	Activity	Outcome / Notes
06:00		
06:30		
07:00		
07:30		
08:00		
08:30		
09:00		
09:30		
10:00		
10:30		
11:00		
11:30		
12:00		
12:30		
13:00		
13:30		
14:00		
14:30		
15:00		
15:30		
16:00		
16:30		
17:00		
17:30		
18:00		
18:30		
19:00		
19:30		
20:00		
20:30		
21:00		

Daily I AMs

I AM
I AM
I AM
I AM
I AM

Tasks I have to do today which contribute to my quarter goals

1.
2.
3.
4.
5.
6.

PRIORITY FOLLOW UP CALL/EMAIL

1.
2.
3.
4.
5.
6.

OTHER TASKS / OR TO DELEGATE

1.
2.
3.
4.
5.

Every day wake up with a purpose.

Daily Play Book.

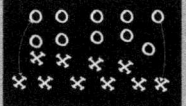

Time	Activity	Outcome / Notes
06:00		
06:30		
07:00		
07:30		
08:00		
08:30		
09:00		
09:30		
10:00		
10:30		
11:00		
11:30		
12:00		
12:30		
13:00		
13:30		
14:00		
14:30		
15:00		
15:30		
16:00		
16:30		
17:00		
17:30		
18:00		
18:30		
19:00		
19:30		
20:00		
20:30		
21:00		

Date:

Daily I AMs

I AM

I AM

I AM

I AM

I AM

Tasks I have to do today which contribute to my quarter goals

1.
2.
3.
4.
5.
6.

PRIORITY FOLLOW UP CALL/EMAIL

1.
2.
3.
4.
5.
6.

OTHER TASKS / OR TO DELEGATE

1.
2.
3.
4.
5.

Be dynamic at all times. Whether in front of adults or the youth. I bring all that I am and give all that I got.

Daily Play Book.

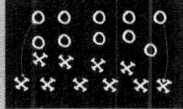

Date:

Time	Activity	Outcome / Notes
06:00		
06:30		
07:00		
07:30		
08:00		
08:30		
09:00		
09:30		
10:00		
10:30		
11:00		
11:30		
12:00		
12:30		
13:00		
13:30		
14:00		
14:30		
15:00		
15:30		
16:00		
16:30		
17:00		
17:30		
18:00		
18:30		
19:00		
19:30		
20:00		
20:30		
21:00		

Daily I AMs

I AM
I AM
I AM
I AM
I AM

Tasks I have to do today which contribute to my quarter goals

1.
2.
3.
4.
5.
6.

PRIORITY FOLLOW UP CALL/EMAIL

1.
2.
3.
4.
5.
6.

OTHER TASKS / OR TO DELEGATE

1.
2.
3.
4.
5.

My life is my Testimony. I choose to tell my story. I'm here to inspire.

Weekly Summary

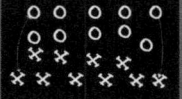

WEEKLY SUMMARY SCORING	Score 1 -10
My focus on TOP weekly priorities...	
My Self Management Time Discipline	
Level of Activity	
Time on Goals	
Self Development	
Health	

BEST PART OF THE WEEK/WHERE I WAS OUTSTANDING & HOW I CELEBRATED
-
-
-

TOP LEARNINGS THIS WEEK
-
-
-

TOP CHALLENGES
-
-
-

TOP FOCUS FOR NEXT WEEK
-
-
-

I AM GRATEFUL FOR
-
-
-

Weekly Playbook Focus Sheet

Name:_____

Weekending:_____   Date:_____ /_____ /_____

*The Number 1 Thing I Must Achieve This Week: _____

*Goals & Actions before next week:	Goal Achieved?	Comments:
Goal 1	☐Yes ☐No	
Goal 2	☐Yes ☐No	
Goal 3	☐Yes ☐No	
Goal 4	☐Yes ☐No	

My brightest achievement in the week just past:

My main challenge during the week gone:

Something that I learned through reading, listening to a tape, watching a video or living life:

At the moment, my greatest focus in life is:

I can find help by :

Briefly speaking :

☐ I spent _____ hrs. working ON myself this last week

☐ My motivation level is at _____ %

☐ Life is _____

I've concentrated on:

☐ Health

☐ Education

☐ Income

☐ Love

☐ Spirituality

I've also worked on:

☐ Relationships

☐ Communication

☐ Planning

☐ Leadership

☐ Best Effort

Daily Play Book.

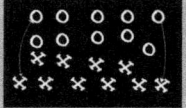

Time	Activity	Outcome / Notes
06:00		
06:30		
07:00		
07:30		
08:00		
08:30		
09:00		
09:30		
10:00		
10:30		
11:00		
11:30		
12:00		
12:30		
13:00		
13:30		
14:00		
14:30		
15:00		
15:30		
16:00		
16:30		
17:00		
17:30		
18:00		
18:30		
19:00		
19:30		
20:00		
20:30		
21:00		

Date:

Daily I AMs

I AM

I AM

I AM

I AM

I AM

Tasks I have to do today which contribute to my quarter goals

1.
2.
3.
4.
5.
6.

PRIORITY FOLLOW UP CALL/EMAIL

1.
2.
3.
4.
5.
6.

OTHER TASKS / OR TO DELEGATE

1.
2.
3.
4.
5.

A great speaker always has something to say.

Daily Play Book.

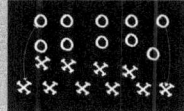

Date:

Time	Activity	Outcome / Notes
06:00		
06:30		
07:00		
07:30		
08:00		
08:30		
09:00		
09:30		
10:00		
10:30		
11:00		
11:30		
12:00		
12:30		
13:00		
13:30		
14:00		
14:30		
15:00		
15:30		
16:00		
16:30		
17:00		
17:30		
18:00		
18:30		
19:00		
19:30		
20:00		
20:30		
21:00		

Daily I AMs

I AM
I AM
I AM
I AM
I AM

Tasks I have to do today which contribute to my quarter goals

1.
2.
3.
4.
5.
6.

PRIORITY FOLLOW UP CALL/EMAIL

1.
2.
3.
4.
5.
6.

OTHER TASKS / OR TO DELEGATE

1.
2.
3.
4.
5.

STILL TRYING TO MAKE MY PARENTS PROUD.

Daily Play Book.

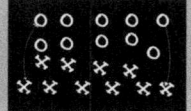

Time	Activity	Outcome / Notes
06:00		
06:30		
07:00		
07:30		
08:00		
08:30		
09:00		
09:30		
10:00		
10:30		
11:00		
11:30		
12:00		
12:30		
13:00		
13:30		
14:00		
14:30		
15:00		
15:30		
16:00		
16:30		
17:00		
17:30		
18:00		
18:30		
19:00		
19:30		
20:00		
20:30		
21:00		

Date:

Daily I AMs

I AM

I AM

I AM

I AM

I AM

Tasks I have to do today which contribute to my quarter goals

1.
2.
3.
4.
5.
6.

PRIORITY FOLLOW UP CALL/EMAIL

1.
2.
3.
4.
5.
6.

OTHER TASKS / OR TO DELEGATE

1.
2.
3.
4.
5.

Life is beautiful. It always gives us something to live for.

Daily Play Book.

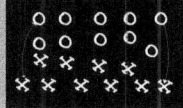

Time	Activity	Outcome / Notes
06:00		
06:30		
07:00		
07:30		
08:00		
08:30		
09:00		
09:30		
10:00		
10:30		
11:00		
11:30		
12:00		
12:30		
13:00		
13:30		
14:00		
14:30		
15:00		
15:30		
16:00		
16:30		
17:00		
17:30		
18:00		
18:30		
19:00		
19:30		
20:00		
20:30		
21:00		

Date:

Daily I AMs

I AM

I AM

I AM

I AM

I AM

Tasks I have to do today which contribute to my quarter goals

1.
2.
3.
4.
5.
6.

PRIORITY FOLLOW UP CALL/EMAIL

1.
2.
3.
4.
5.
6.

OTHER TASKS / OR TO DELEGATE

1.
2.
3.
4.
5.

Woke up to my conscience asking, "HOW IMPORTANT IS IT TO YOU, THAT YOU REACH YOUR FULLEST POTENTIAL?"

Daily Play Book.

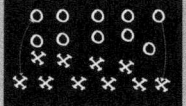

Time	Activity	Outcome / Notes
06:00		
06:30		
07:00		
07:30		
08:00		
08:30		
09:00		
09:30		
10:00		
10:30		
11:00		
11:30		
12:00		
12:30		
13:00		
13:30		
14:00		
14:30		
15:00		
15:30		
16:00		
16:30		
17:00		
17:30		
18:00		
18:30		
19:00		
19:30		
20:00		
20:30		
21:00		

Date:

Daily I AMs

I AM

I AM

I AM

I AM

I AM

Tasks I have to do today which contribute to my quarter goals

1.
2.
3.
4.
5.
6.

PRIORITY FOLLOW UP CALL/EMAIL

1.
2.
3.
4.
5.
6.

OTHER TASKS / OR TO DELEGATE

1.
2.
3.
4.
5.

"You have to plan for success." Or else it will be a one hit wonder.

Daily Play Book.

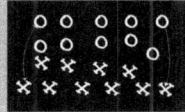

Date:

Time	Activity	Outcome / Notes
06:00		
06:30		
07:00		
07:30		
08:00		
08:30		
09:00		
09:30		
10:00		
10:30		
11:00		
11:30		
12:00		
12:30		
13:00		
13:30		
14:00		
14:30		
15:00		
15:30		
16:00		
16:30		
17:00		
17:30		
18:00		
18:30		
19:00		
19:30		
20:00		
20:30		
21:00		

Daily I AMs

I AM

I AM

I AM

I AM

I AM

Tasks I have to do today which contribute to my quarter goals

1.
2.
3.
4.
5.
6.

PRIORITY FOLLOW UP CALL/EMAIL

1.
2.
3.
4.
5.
6.

OTHER TASKS / OR TO DELEGATE

1.
2.
3.
4.
5.

Some people would rather get even than to get ahead. Stay focused on your destiny, "no one" is worth your dream.

Daily Play Book.

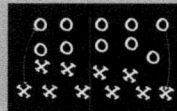

Time	Activity	Outcome / Notes
06:00		
06:30		
07:00		
07:30		
08:00		
08:30		
09:00		
09:30		
10:00		
10:30		
11:00		
11:30		
12:00		
12:30		
13:00		
13:30		
14:00		
14:30		
15:00		
15:30		
16:00		
16:30		
17:00		
17:30		
18:00		
18:30		
19:00		
19:30		
20:00		
20:30		
21:00		

Date:

Daily I AMs

I AM

I AM

I AM

I AM

I AM

Tasks I have to do today which contribute to my quarter goals

1.
2.
3.
4.
5.
6.

PRIORITY FOLLOW UP CALL/EMAIL

1.
2.
3.
4.
5.
6.

OTHER TASKS / OR TO DELEGATE

1.
2.
3.
4.
5.

Avoid paths that are full of traps. When you arm the mind with knowledge you can see the trouble ahead. When you align with spirit, you can sense it.

Weekly Summary

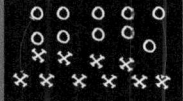

WEEKLY SUMMARY SCORING	Score 1 -10
My focus on TOP weekly priorities...	
My Self Management Time Discipline	
Level of Activity	
Time on Goals	
Self Development	
Health	

BEST PART OF THE WEEK/WHERE I WAS OUTSTANDING & HOW I CELEBRATED
•
•
•

TOP LEARNINGS THIS WEEK
•
•
•

TOP CHALLENGES
•
•
•

TOP FOCUS FOR NEXT WEEK
•
•
•

I AM GRATEFUL FOR
•
•
•

Weekly Playbook Focus Sheet

Name:_____

Weekending:_____   Date:_____ /_____ /_____

*The Number 1 Thing I Must Achieve This Week: _____

*Goals & Actions before next week:	Goal Achieved?	Comments:
Goal 1	☐Yes ☐No	
Goal 2	☐Yes ☐No	
Goal 3	☐Yes ☐No	
Goal 4	☐Yes ☐No	

My brightest achievement in the week just past:

My main challenge during the week gone:

Something that I learned through reading, listening to a tape, watching a video or living life:

At the moment, my greatest focus in life is:

I can find help by :

Briefly speaking :	I've concentrated on:	I've also worked on:
☐ I spent _____ hrs. working ON myself this last week	☐ Health	☐ Relationships
☐ My motivation level is at _____ %	☐ Education	☐ Communication
☐ Life is _____	☐ Income	☐ Planning
	☐ Love	☐ Leadership
	☐ Spirituality	☐ Best Effort

Daily Play Book.

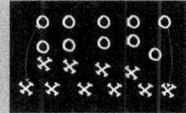

Time	Activity	Outcome / Notes
06:00		
06:30		
07:00		
07:30		
08:00		
08:30		
09:00		
09:30		
10:00		
10:30		
11:00		
11:30		
12:00		
12:30		
13:00		
13:30		
14:00		
14:30		
15:00		
15:30		
16:00		
16:30		
17:00		
17:30		
18:00		
18:30		
19:00		
19:30		
20:00		
20:30		
21:00		

Date:

Daily I AMs

I AM
I AM
I AM
I AM
I AM

Tasks I have to do today which contribute to my quarter goals

1.
2.
3.
4.
5.
6.

PRIORITY FOLLOW UP CALL/EMAIL

1.
2.
3.
4.
5.
6.

OTHER TASKS / OR TO DELEGATE

1.
2.
3.
4.
5.

Better than yesterday.

Daily Play Book.

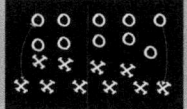

Date:

Time	Activity	Outcome / Notes
06:00		
06:30		
07:00		
07:30		
08:00		
08:30		
09:00		
09:30		
10:00		
10:30		
11:00		
11:30		
12:00		
12:30		
13:00		
13:30		
14:00		
14:30		
15:00		
15:30		
16:00		
16:30		
17:00		
17:30		
18:00		
18:30		
19:00		
19:30		
20:00		
20:30		
21:00		

Daily I AMs

I AM
I AM
I AM
I AM
I AM

Tasks I have to do today which contribute to my quarter goals

1.
2.
3.
4.
5.
6.

PRIORITY FOLLOW UP CALL/EMAIL

1.
2.
3.
4.
5.
6.

OTHER TASKS / OR TO DELEGATE

1.
2.
3.
4.
5.

It is all coming together. Patience, vision, and effort.

Daily Play Book.

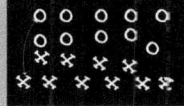

Date:

Time	Activity	Outcome / Notes
06:00		
06:30		
07:00		
07:30		
08:00		
08:30		
09:00		
09:30		
10:00		
10:30		
11:00		
11:30		
12:00		
12:30		
13:00		
13:30		
14:00		
14:30		
15:00		
15:30		
16:00		
16:30		
17:00		
17:30		
18:00		
18:30		
19:00		
19:30		
20:00		
20:30		
21:00		

Daily I AMs

I AM

I AM

I AM

I AM

I AM

Tasks I have to do today which contribute to my quarter goals

1.

2.

3.

4.

5.

6.

PRIORITY FOLLOW UP CALL/EMAIL

1.

2.

3.

4.

5.

6.

OTHER TASKS / OR TO DELEGATE

1.

2.

3.

4.

5.

Sometimes you must remove people from your corner so that God can take his position. Once God is there you are no longer in control. God will coach and direct you, but YOU must fight the fight. Be obedient and you will never SUFFER in defeat.

Daily Play Book.

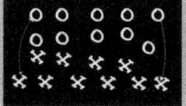

Time	Activity	Outcome / Notes
06:00		
06:30		
07:00		
07:30		
08:00		
08:30		
09:00		
09:30		
10:00		
10:30		
11:00		
11:30		
12:00		
12:30		
13:00		
13:30		
14:00		
14:30		
15:00		
15:30		
16:00		
16:30		
17:00		
17:30		
18:00		
18:30		
19:00		
19:30		
20:00		
20:30		
21:00		

Date:

Daily I AMs

I AM

I AM

I AM

I AM

I AM

Tasks I have to do today which contribute to my quarter goals

1.
2.
3.
4.
5.
6.

PRIORITY FOLLOW UP CALL/EMAIL

1.
2.
3.
4.
5.
6.

OTHER TASKS / OR TO DELEGATE

1.
2.
3.
4.
5.

You do not need a degree to become a Business Owner, but you do need a degree to work for one.

Daily Play Book.

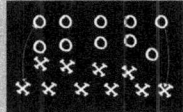

Date:

Time	Activity	Outcome / Notes
06:00		
06:30		
07:00		
07:30		
08:00		
08:30		
09:00		
09:30		
10:00		
10:30		
11:00		
11:30		
12:00		
12:30		
13:00		
13:30		
14:00		
14:30		
15:00		
15:30		
16:00		
16:30		
17:00		
17:30		
18:00		
18:30		
19:00		
19:30		
20:00		
20:30		
21:00		

Daily I AMs

I AM

I AM

I AM

I AM

I AM

Tasks I have to do today which contribute to my quarter goals

1.
2.
3.
4.
5.
6.

PRIORITY FOLLOW UP CALL/EMAIL

1.
2.
3.
4.
5.
6.

OTHER TASKS / OR TO DELEGATE

1.
2.
3.
4.
5.

One man's discipline is connected to many people's destiny.

Daily Play Book.

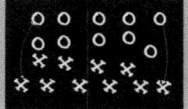

Time	Activity	Outcome / Notes
06:00		
06:30		
07:00		
07:30		
08:00		
08:30		
09:00		
09:30		
10:00		
10:30		
11:00		
11:30		
12:00		
12:30		
13:00		
13:30		
14:00		
14:30		
15:00		
15:30		
16:00		
16:30		
17:00		
17:30		
18:00		
18:30		
19:00		
19:30		
20:00		
20:30		
21:00		

Date:

Daily I AMs

I AM

I AM

I AM

I AM

I AM

Tasks I have to do today which contribute to my quarter goals

1.
2.
3.
4.
5.
6.

PRIORITY FOLLOW UP CALL/EMAIL

1.
2.
3.
4.
5.
6.

OTHER TASKS / OR TO DELEGATE

1.
2.
3.
4.
5.

Do not let them use you.

Daily Play Book.

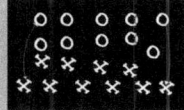

Time	Activity	Outcome / Notes
06:00		
06:30		
07:00		
07:30		
08:00		
08:30		
09:00		
09:30		
10:00		
10:30		
11:00		
11:30		
12:00		
12:30		
13:00		
13:30		
14:00		
14:30		
15:00		
15:30		
16:00		
16:30		
17:00		
17:30		
18:00		
18:30		
19:00		
19:30		
20:00		
20:30		
21:00		

Date:

Daily I AMs

I AM
I AM
I AM
I AM
I AM

Tasks I have to do today which contribute to my quarter goals

1.
2.
3.
4.
5.
6.

PRIORITY FOLLOW UP CALL/EMAIL

1.
2.
3.
4.
5.
6.

OTHER TASKS / OR TO DELEGATE

1.
2.
3.
4.
5.

The goal of the soul is to be free of anger, envy, and greed.

Daily Play Book.

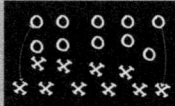

Time	Activity	Outcome / Notes
06:00		
06:30		
07:00		
07:30		
08:00		
08:30		
09:00		
09:30		
10:00		
10:30		
11:00		
11:30		
12:00		
12:30		
13:00		
13:30		
14:00		
14:30		
15:00		
15:30		
16:00		
16:30		
17:00		
17:30		
18:00		
18:30		
19:00		
19:30		
20:00		
20:30		
21:00		

Date:

Daily I AMs
I AM
I AM
I AM
I AM
I AM

Tasks I have to do today which contribute to my quarter goals
1.
2.
3.
4.
5.
6.

PRIORITY FOLLOW UP CALL/EMAIL
1.
2.
3.
4.
5.
6.

OTHER TASKS / OR TO DELEGATE
1.
2.
3.
4.
5.

Success comes from masterminding self-control. Once you control habits and release the restrictions of the mind, what you want becomes accessible.

Daily Play Book.

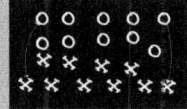

Time	Activity	Outcome / Notes
06:00		
06:30		
07:00		
07:30		
08:00		
08:30		
09:00		
09:30		
10:00		
10:30		
11:00		
11:30		
12:00		
12:30		
13:00		
13:30		
14:00		
14:30		
15:00		
15:30		
16:00		
16:30		
17:00		
17:30		
18:00		
18:30		
19:00		
19:30		
20:00		
20:30		
21:00		

Date:

Daily I AMs

I AM

I AM

I AM

I AM

I AM

Tasks I have to do today which contribute to my quarter goals

1.
2.
3.
4.
5.
6.

PRIORITY FOLLOW UP CALL/EMAIL

1.
2.
3.
4.
5.
6.

OTHER TASKS / OR TO DELEGATE

1.
2.
3.
4.
5.

We must empower, encourage, and love one another.

Weekly Summary

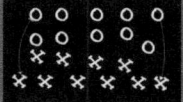

WEEKLY SUMMARY SCORING	Score 1 -10
My focus on TOP weekly priorities...	
My Self Management Time Discipline	
Level of Activity	
Time on Goals	
Self Development	
Health	

BEST PART OF THE WEEK/WHERE I WAS OUTSTANDING & HOW I CELEBRATED
•
•
•

TOP LEARNINGS THIS WEEK
•
•
•

TOP CHALLENGES
•
•
•

TOP FOCUS FOR NEXT WEEK
•
•
•

I AM GRATEFUL FOR
•
•
•

PlayBook Calender

Month:_____   Year:_____

Monday	Tuesday	Wednesday	Thursday	Friday	Saturday	Sunday

Events	Important Dates	Social Events	Meetings

Weekly Playbook Focus Sheet

Name:_____

Weekending:_____   Date:_____ /_____ /_____

*The Number 1 Thing I Must Achieve This Week: _____

*Goals & Actions before next week:	Goal Achieved?	Comments:
Goal 1	☐ Yes ☐ No	
Goal 2	☐ Yes ☐ No	
Goal 3	☐ Yes ☐ No	
Goal 4	☐ Yes ☐ No	

My brightest achievement in the week just past:

My main challenge during the week gone:

Something that I learned through reading, listening to a tape, watching a video or living life:

At the moment, my greatest focus in life is:

I can find help by :

Briefly speaking :

☐ I spent _____ hrs. working ON myself this last week

☐ My motivation level is at _____ %

☐ Life is _____

I've concentrated on:

☐ Health

☐ Education

☐ Income

☐ Love

☐ Spirituality

I've also worked on:

☐ Relationships

☐ Communication

☐ Planning

☐ Leadership

☐ Best Effort

Daily Play Book.

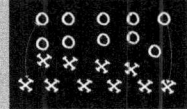

Date:

Time	Activity	Outcome / Notes
06:00		
06:30		
07:00		
07:30		
08:00		
08:30		
09:00		
09:30		
10:00		
10:30		
11:00		
11:30		
12:00		
12:30		
13:00		
13:30		
14:00		
14:30		
15:00		
15:30		
16:00		
16:30		
17:00		
17:30		
18:00		
18:30		
19:00		
19:30		
20:00		
20:30		
21:00		

Daily I AMs

I AM

I AM

I AM

I AM

I AM

Tasks I have to do today which contribute to my quarter goals

1.
2.
3.
4.
5.
6.

PRIORITY FOLLOW UP CALL/EMAIL

1.
2.
3.
4.
5.
6.

OTHER TASKS / OR TO DELEGATE

1.
2.
3.
4.
5.

When your unable to change your environment, clean it.

Daily Play Book.

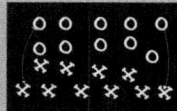

Time	Activity	Outcome / Notes
06:00		
06:30		
07:00		
07:30		
08:00		
08:30		
09:00		
09:30		
10:00		
10:30		
11:00		
11:30		
12:00		
12:30		
13:00		
13:30		
14:00		
14:30		
15:00		
15:30		
16:00		
16:30		
17:00		
17:30		
18:00		
18:30		
19:00		
19:30		
20:00		
20:30		
21:00		

Date:

Daily I AMs

I AM
I AM
I AM
I AM
I AM

Tasks I have to do today which contribute to my quarter goals

1.
2.
3.
4.
5.
6.

PRIORITY FOLLOW UP CALL/EMAIL

1.
2.
3.
4.
5.
6.

OTHER TASKS / OR TO DELEGATE

1.
2.
3.
4.
5.

Be careful what you think about.

Daily Play Book.

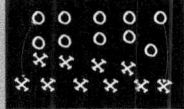

Time	Activity	Outcome / Notes
06:00		
06:30		
07:00		
07:30		
08:00		
08:30		
09:00		
09:30		
10:00		
10:30		
11:00		
11:30		
12:00		
12:30		
13:00		
13:30		
14:00		
14:30		
15:00		
15:30		
16:00		
16:30		
17:00		
17:30		
18:00		
18:30		
19:00		
19:30		
20:00		
20:30		
21:00		

Date:

Daily I AMs

I AM

I AM

I AM

I AM

I AM

Tasks I have to do today which contribute to my quarter goals

1.
2.
3.
4.
5.
6.

PRIORITY FOLLOW UP CALL/EMAIL

1.
2.
3.
4.
5.
6.

OTHER TASKS / OR TO DELEGATE

1.
2.
3.
4.
5.

"It's amazing how sometimes we have to force ourselves to do what's good for us."

Daily Play Book.

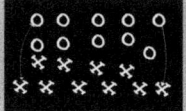

Time	Activity	Outcome / Notes
06:00		
06:30		
07:00		
07:30		
08:00		
08:30		
09:00		
09:30		
10:00		
10:30		
11:00		
11:30		
12:00		
12:30		
13:00		
13:30		
14:00		
14:30		
15:00		
15:30		
16:00		
16:30		
17:00		
17:30		
18:00		
18:30		
19:00		
19:30		
20:00		
20:30		
21:00		

Date:

Daily I AMs

I AM
I AM
I AM
I AM
I AM

Tasks I have to do today which contribute to my quarter goals

1.
2.
3.
4.
5.
6.

PRIORITY FOLLOW UP CALL/EMAIL

1.
2.
3.
4.
5.
6.

OTHER TASKS / OR TO DELEGATE

1.
2.
3.
4.
5.

Evolve with the Climate. No one can stop it.

Daily Play Book.

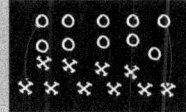

Time	Activity	Outcome / Notes
06:00		
06:30		
07:00		
07:30		
08:00		
08:30		
09:00		
09:30		
10:00		
10:30		
11:00		
11:30		
12:00		
12:30		
13:00		
13:30		
14:00		
14:30		
15:00		
15:30		
16:00		
16:30		
17:00		
17:30		
18:00		
18:30		
19:00		
19:30		
20:00		
20:30		
21:00		

Date:

Daily I AMs

I AM
I AM
I AM
I AM
I AM

Tasks I have to do today which contribute to my quarter goals

1.
2.
3.
4.
5.
6.

PRIORITY FOLLOW UP CALL/EMAIL

1.
2.
3.
4.
5.
6.

OTHER TASKS / OR TO DELEGATE

1.
2.
3.
4.
5.

"There are no short cuts in life, but with the right strategy and systems in place, we minimize mistakes and the wasting of time."

Daily Play Book.

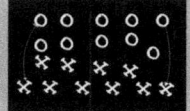

Time	Activity	Outcome / Notes
06:00		
06:30		
07:00		
07:30		
08:00		
08:30		
09:00		
09:30		
10:00		
10:30		
11:00		
11:30		
12:00		
12:30		
13:00		
13:30		
14:00		
14:30		
15:00		
15:30		
16:00		
16:30		
17:00		
17:30		
18:00		
18:30		
19:00		
19:30		
20:00		
20:30		
21:00		

Date:

Daily I AMs

I AM

I AM

I AM

I AM

I AM

Tasks I have to do today which contribute to my quarter goals

1.
2.
3.
4.
5.
6.

PRIORITY FOLLOW UP CALL/EMAIL

1.
2.
3.
4.
5.
6.

OTHER TASKS / OR TO DELEGATE

1.
2.
3.
4.
5.

"Regardless what happened, you are responsible for you and your journey."

Daily Play Book.

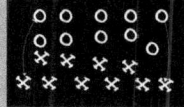

Time	Activity	Outcome / Notes
06:00		
06:30		
07:00		
07:30		
08:00		
08:30		
09:00		
09:30		
10:00		
10:30		
11:00		
11:30		
12:00		
12:30		
13:00		
13:30		
14:00		
14:30		
15:00		
15:30		
16:00		
16:30		
17:00		
17:30		
18:00		
18:30		
19:00		
19:30		
20:00		
20:30		
21:00		

Date:

Daily I AMs

I AM

I AM

I AM

I AM

I AM

Tasks I have to do today which contribute to my quarter goals

1.
2.
3.
4.
5.
6.

PRIORITY FOLLOW UP CALL/EMAIL

1.
2.
3.
4.
5.
6.

OTHER TASKS / OR TO DELEGATE

1.
2.
3.
4.
5.

When you stop believing in yourself the enemy has won.

Weekly Summary

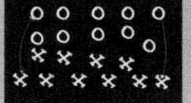

WEEKLY SUMMARY SCORING	Score 1-10
My focus on TOP weekly priorities...	
My Self Management Time Discipline	
Level of Activity	
Time on Goals	
Self Development	
Health	

BEST PART OF THE WEEK/WHERE I WAS OUTSTANDING & HOW I CELEBRATED
•
•
•

TOP LEARNINGS THIS WEEK
•
•
•

TOP CHALLENGES
•
•
•

TOP FOCUS FOR NEXT WEEK
•
•
•

I AM GRATEFUL FOR
•
•
•

Weekly Playbook Focus Sheet

Name:_____

Weekending:_____   Date:_____ /_____ /_____

*The Number 1 Thing I Must Achieve This Week: _____

*Goals & Actions before next week:	Goal Achieved?	Comments:
Goal 1	☐ Yes ☐ No	
Goal 2	☐ Yes ☐ No	
Goal 3	☐ Yes ☐ No	
Goal 4	☐ Yes ☐ No	

My brightest achievement in the week just past:

My main challenge during the week gone:

Something that I learned through reading, listening to a tape, watching a video or living life:

At the moment, my greatest focus in life is:

I can find help by :

Briefly speaking :

☐ I spent _____ hrs. working ON myself this last week

☐ My motivation level is at _____ %

☐ Life is _____

I've concentrated on:

☐ Health

☐ Education

☐ Income

☐ Love

☐ Spirituality

I've also worked on:

☐ Relationships

☐ Communication

☐ Planning

☐ Leadership

☐ Best Effort

Daily Play Book.

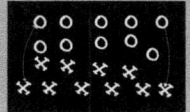

Time	Activity	Outcome / Notes
06:00		
06:30		
07:00		
07:30		
08:00		
08:30		
09:00		
09:30		
10:00		
10:30		
11:00		
11:30		
12:00		
12:30		
13:00		
13:30		
14:00		
14:30		
15:00		
15:30		
16:00		
16:30		
17:00		
17:30		
18:00		
18:30		
19:00		
19:30		
20:00		
20:30		
21:00		

Date:

Daily I AMs

I AM

I AM

I AM

I AM

I AM

Tasks I have to do today which contribute to my quarter goals

1.
2.
3.
4.
5.
6.

PRIORITY FOLLOW UP CALL/EMAIL

1.
2.
3.
4.
5.
6.

OTHER TASKS / OR TO DELEGATE

1.
2.
3.
4.
5.

When there is no peace around you, search within.

Daily Play Book.

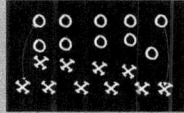

Time	Activity	Outcome / Notes
06:00		
06:30		
07:00		
07:30		
08:00		
08:30		
09:00		
09:30		
10:00		
10:30		
11:00		
11:30		
12:00		
12:30		
13:00		
13:30		
14:00		
14:30		
15:00		
15:30		
16:00		
16:30		
17:00		
17:30		
18:00		
18:30		
19:00		
19:30		
20:00		
20:30		
21:00		

Date:

Daily I AMs

I AM
I AM
I AM
I AM
I AM

Tasks I have to do today which contribute to my quarter goals

1.
2.
3.
4.
5.
6.

PRIORITY FOLLOW UP CALL/EMAIL

1.
2.
3.
4.
5.
6.

OTHER TASKS / OR TO DELEGATE

1.
2.
3.
4.
5.

No such thing as a life that is better than yours.

Daily Play Book.

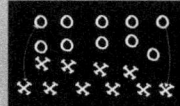

Time	Activity	Outcome / Notes
06:00		
06:30		
07:00		
07:30		
08:00		
08:30		
09:00		
09:30		
10:00		
10:30		
11:00		
11:30		
12:00		
12:30		
13:00		
13:30		
14:00		
14:30		
15:00		
15:30		
16:00		
16:30		
17:00		
17:30		
18:00		
18:30		
19:00		
19:30		
20:00		
20:30		
21:00		

Date:

Daily I AMs

I AM

I AM

I AM

I AM

I AM

Tasks I have to do today which contribute to my quarter goals

1.
2.
3.
4.
5.
6.

PRIORITY FOLLOW UP CALL/EMAIL

1.
2.
3.
4.
5.
6.

OTHER TASKS / OR TO DELEGATE

1.
2.
3.
4.
5.

Love Yours, #jcole

Daily Play Book.

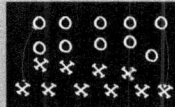

Time	Activity	Outcome / Notes
06:00		
06:30		
07:00		
07:30		
08:00		
08:30		
09:00		
09:30		
10:00		
10:30		
11:00		
11:30		
12:00		
12:30		
13:00		
13:30		
14:00		
14:30		
15:00		
15:30		
16:00		
16:30		
17:00		
17:30		
18:00		
18:30		
19:00		
19:30		
20:00		
20:30		
21:00		

Date:

Daily I AMs

I AM
I AM
I AM
I AM
I AM

Tasks I have to do today which contribute to my quarter goals

1.
2.
3.
4.
5.
6.

PRIORITY FOLLOW UP CALL/EMAIL

1.
2.
3.
4.
5.
6.

OTHER TASKS / OR TO DELEGATE

1.
2.
3.
4.
5.

When you cannot find a mentor, find a book.

Daily Play Book.

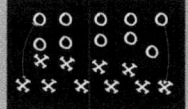

Time	Activity	Outcome / Notes
06:00		
06:30		
07:00		
07:30		
08:00		
08:30		
09:00		
09:30		
10:00		
10:30		
11:00		
11:30		
12:00		
12:30		
13:00		
13:30		
14:00		
14:30		
15:00		
15:30		
16:00		
16:30		
17:00		
17:30		
18:00		
18:30		
19:00		
19:30		
20:00		
20:30		
21:00		

Date:

Daily I AMs

I AM

I AM

I AM

I AM

I AM

Tasks I have to do today which contribute to my quarter goals

1.
2.
3.
4.
5.
6.

PRIORITY FOLLOW UP CALL/EMAIL

1.
2.
3.
4.
5.
6.

OTHER TASKS / OR TO DELEGATE

1.
2.
3.
4.
5.

The foundation to my purpose is the gifts I have been given.

Daily Play Book.

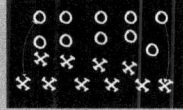

Time	Activity	Outcome / Notes
06:00		
06:30		
07:00		
07:30		
08:00		
08:30		
09:00		
09:30		
10:00		
10:30		
11:00		
11:30		
12:00		
12:30		
13:00		
13:30		
14:00		
14:30		
15:00		
15:30		
16:00		
16:30		
17:00		
17:30		
18:00		
18:30		
19:00		
19:30		
20:00		
20:30		
21:00		

Date:

Daily I AMs

I AM

I AM

I AM

I AM

I AM

Tasks I have to do today which contribute to my quarter goals

1.
2.
3.
4.
5.
6.

PRIORITY FOLLOW UP CALL/EMAIL

1.
2.
3.
4.
5.
6.

OTHER TASKS / OR TO DELEGATE

1.
2.
3.
4.
5.

LOVE

Daily Play Book.

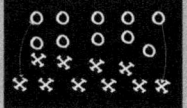

Time	Activity	Outcome / Notes
06:00		
06:30		
07:00		
07:30		
08:00		
08:30		
09:00		
09:30		
10:00		
10:30		
11:00		
11:30		
12:00		
12:30		
13:00		
13:30		
14:00		
14:30		
15:00		
15:30		
16:00		
16:30		
17:00		
17:30		
18:00		
18:30		
19:00		
19:30		
20:00		
20:30		
21:00		

Date:

Daily I AMs

I AM

I AM

I AM

I AM

I AM

Tasks I have to do today which contribute to my quarter goals

1.

2.

3.

4.

5.

6.

PRIORITY FOLLOW UP CALL/EMAIL

1.

2.

3.

4.

5.

6.

OTHER TASKS / OR TO DELEGATE

1.

2.

3.

4.

5.

Champions are created in the Early AM hours, while majority of the world is asleep or deprived.

Weekly Summary

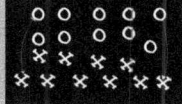

WEEKLY SUMMARY SCORING	Score 1 -10
My focus on TOP weekly priorities...	
My Self Management Time Discipline	
Level of Activity	
Time on Goals	
Self Development	
Health	

BEST PART OF THE WEEK/WHERE I WAS OUTSTANDING & HOW I CELEBRATED

-
-
-

TOP LEARNINGS THIS WEEK

-
-
-

TOP CHALLENGES

-
-
-

TOP FOCUS FOR NEXT WEEK

-
-
-

I AM GRATEFUL FOR

-
-
-

Weekly Playbook Focus Sheet

Name:_____

Weekending:_____   Date:_____ /_____ /_____

*The Number 1 Thing I Must Achieve This Week: _____

*Goals & Actions before next week:		Goal Achieved?	Comments:
Goal 1		☐Yes ☐No	
Goal 2		☐Yes ☐No	
Goal 3		☐Yes ☐No	
Goal 4		☐Yes ☐No	

My brightest achievement in the week just past:

My main challenge during the week gone:

Something that I learned through reading, listening to a tape, watching a video or living life:

At the moment, my greatest focus in life is:

I can find help by :

Briefly speaking :	I've concentrated on:	I've also worked on:
☐ I spent _____ hrs. working ON myself this last week	☐ Health	☐ Relationships
☐ My motivation level is at _____ %	☐ Education	☐ Communication
☐ Life is _____	☐ Income	☐ Planning
	☐ Love	☐ Leadership
	☐ Spirituality	☐ Best Effort

Daily Play Book.

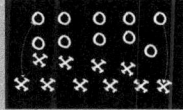

Date:

Time	Activity	Outcome / Notes
06:00		
06:30		
07:00		
07:30		
08:00		
08:30		
09:00		
09:30		
10:00		
10:30		
11:00		
11:30		
12:00		
12:30		
13:00		
13:30		
14:00		
14:30		
15:00		
15:30		
16:00		
16:30		
17:00		
17:30		
18:00		
18:30		
19:00		
19:30		
20:00		
20:30		
21:00		

Daily I AMs

I AM
I AM
I AM
I AM
I AM

Tasks I have to do today which contribute to my quarter goals

1.
2.
3.
4.
5.
6.

PRIORITY FOLLOW UP CALL/EMAIL

1.
2.
3.
4.
5.
6.

OTHER TASKS / OR TO DELEGATE

1.
2.
3.
4.
5.

But please believe I will be taking a 1-hour nap.

Daily Play Book.

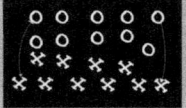

Time	Activity	Outcome / Notes
06:00		
06:30		
07:00		
07:30		
08:00		
08:30		
09:00		
09:30		
10:00		
10:30		
11:00		
11:30		
12:00		
12:30		
13:00		
13:30		
14:00		
14:30		
15:00		
15:30		
16:00		
16:30		
17:00		
17:30		
18:00		
18:30		
19:00		
19:30		
20:00		
20:30		
21:00		

Date:

Daily I AMs

I AM
I AM
I AM
I AM
I AM

Tasks I have to do today which contribute to my quarter goals

1.
2.
3.
4.
5.
6.

PRIORITY FOLLOW UP CALL/EMAIL

1.
2.
3.
4.
5.
6.

OTHER TASKS / OR TO DELEGATE

1.
2.
3.
4.
5.

*Be so happy that people hate on you,
because your too happy! :)*

Daily Play Book.

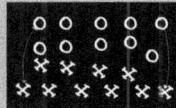

Date:

Time	Activity	Outcome / Notes
06:00		
06:30		
07:00		
07:30		
08:00		
08:30		
09:00		
09:30		
10:00		
10:30		
11:00		
11:30		
12:00		
12:30		
13:00		
13:30		
14:00		
14:30		
15:00		
15:30		
16:00		
16:30		
17:00		
17:30		
18:00		
18:30		
19:00		
19:30		
20:00		
20:30		
21:00		

Daily I AMs

I AM
I AM
I AM
I AM
I AM

Tasks I have to do today which contribute to my quarter goals

1.
2.
3.
4.
5.
6.

PRIORITY FOLLOW UP CALL/EMAIL

1.
2.
3.
4.
5.
6.

OTHER TASKS / OR TO DELEGATE

1.
2.
3.
4.
5.

Did you know 95% of people cannot lick their elbow?

Daily Play Book.

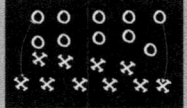

Time	Activity	Outcome / Notes
06:00		
06:30		
07:00		
07:30		
08:00		
08:30		
09:00		
09:30		
10:00		
10:30		
11:00		
11:30		
12:00		
12:30		
13:00		
13:30		
14:00		
14:30		
15:00		
15:30		
16:00		
16:30		
17:00		
17:30		
18:00		
18:30		
19:00		
19:30		
20:00		
20:30		
21:00		

Date:

Daily I AMs

I AM

I AM

I AM

I AM

I AM

Tasks I have to do today which contribute to my quarter goals

1.
2.
3.
4.
5.
6.

PRIORITY FOLLOW UP CALL/EMAIL

1.
2.
3.
4.
5.
6.

OTHER TASKS / OR TO DELEGATE

1.
2.
3.
4.
5.

Be careful where you look for love and acceptance.

Daily Play Book.

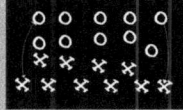

Time	Activity	Outcome / Notes
06:00		
06:30		
07:00		
07:30		
08:00		
08:30		
09:00		
09:30		
10:00		
10:30		
11:00		
11:30		
12:00		
12:30		
13:00		
13:30		
14:00		
14:30		
15:00		
15:30		
16:00		
16:30		
17:00		
17:30		
18:00		
18:30		
19:00		
19:30		
20:00		
20:30		
21:00		

Date:

Daily I AMs

I AM

I AM

I AM

I AM

I AM

Tasks I have to do today which contribute to my quarter goals

1.
2.
3.
4.
5.
6.

PRIORITY FOLLOW UP CALL/EMAIL

1.
2.
3.
4.
5.
6.

OTHER TASKS / OR TO DELEGATE

1.
2.
3.
4.
5.

Make someone smile today, and I guarantee you someone will make you do the same. So why not everybody?

Daily Play Book.

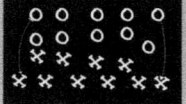

Time	Activity	Outcome / Notes
06:00		
06:30		
07:00		
07:30		
08:00		
08:30		
09:00		
09:30		
10:00		
10:30		
11:00		
11:30		
12:00		
12:30		
13:00		
13:30		
14:00		
14:30		
15:00		
15:30		
16:00		
16:30		
17:00		
17:30		
18:00		
18:30		
19:00		
19:30		
20:00		
20:30		
21:00		

Date:

Daily I AMs

I AM

I AM

I AM

I AM

I AM

Tasks I have to do today which contribute to my quarter goals

1.
2.
3.
4.
5.
6.

PRIORITY FOLLOW UP CALL/EMAIL

1.
2.
3.
4.
5.
6.

OTHER TASKS / OR TO DELEGATE

1.
2.
3.
4.
5.

People who do not study, fear learning what they need to change.

Daily Play Book.

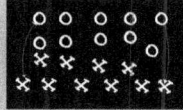

Time	Activity	Outcome / Notes
06:00		
06:30		
07:00		
07:30		
08:00		
08:30		
09:00		
09:30		
10:00		
10:30		
11:00		
11:30		
12:00		
12:30		
13:00		
13:30		
14:00		
14:30		
15:00		
15:30		
16:00		
16:30		
17:00		
17:30		
18:00		
18:30		
19:00		
19:30		
20:00		
20:30		
21:00		

Date:

Daily I AMs

I AM

I AM

I AM

I AM

I AM

Tasks I have to do today which contribute to my quarter goals

1.
2.
3.
4.
5.
6.

PRIORITY FOLLOW UP CALL/EMAIL

1.
2.
3.
4.
5.
6.

OTHER TASKS / OR TO DELEGATE

1.
2.
3.
4.
5.

People who have supernatural potential, but lack morality, always fall. Oh, have I been humbled.

Weekly Summary

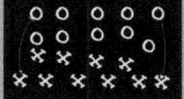

WEEKLY SUMMARY SCORING	Score 1 -10
My focus on TOP weekly priorities...	
My Self Management Time Discipline	
Level of Activity	
Time on Goals	
Self Development	
Health	

BEST PART OF THE WEEK/WHERE I WAS OUTSTANDING & HOW I CELEBRATED
-
-
-

TOP LEARNINGS THIS WEEK
-
-
-

TOP CHALLENGES
-
-
-

TOP FOCUS FOR NEXT WEEK
-
-
-

I AM GRATEFUL FOR
-
-
-

Weekly Playbook Focus Sheet

Name:_____

Weekending:_____   Date:_____ /_____ /_____

*The Number 1 Thing I Must Achieve This Week: _____

*Goals & Actions before next week:	Goal Achieved?	Comments:
Goal 1	☐ Yes ☐ No	
Goal 2	☐ Yes ☐ No	
Goal 3	☐ Yes ☐ No	
Goal 4	☐ Yes ☐ No	

My brightest achievement in the week just past:

My main challenge during the week gone:

Something that I learned through reading, listening to a tape, watching a video or living life:

At the moment, my greatest focus in life is:

I can find help by :

Briefly speaking :   I've concentrated on: I've also worked on:

☐ I spent _____ hrs.   ☐ Health   ☐ Relationships
  working ON myself this last
  week   ☐ Education   ☐ Communication

☐ My motivation level is at   ☐ Income   ☐ Planning
  _____ %
                                     ☐ Love   ☐ Leadership
☐ Life is _____
                                     ☐ Spirituality   ☐ Best Effort

Daily Play Book.

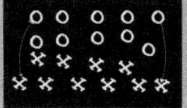

Time	Activity	Outcome / Notes
06:00		
06:30		
07:00		
07:30		
08:00		
08:30		
09:00		
09:30		
10:00		
10:30		
11:00		
11:30		
12:00		
12:30		
13:00		
13:30		
14:00		
14:30		
15:00		
15:30		
16:00		
16:30		
17:00		
17:30		
18:00		
18:30		
19:00		
19:30		
20:00		
20:30		
21:00		

Date:

Daily I AMs

I AM

I AM

I AM

I AM

I AM

Tasks I have to do today which contribute to my quarter goals

1.
2.
3.
4.
5.
6.

PRIORITY FOLLOW UP CALL/EMAIL

1.
2.
3.
4.
5.
6.

OTHER TASKS / OR TO DELEGATE

1.
2.
3.
4.
5.

When others are aligned on your purpose, you must take heed of the energy around you and what your capable of as a team.

Daily Play Book.

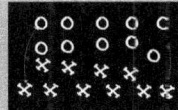

Time	Activity	Outcome / Notes
06:00		
06:30		
07:00		
07:30		
08:00		
08:30		
09:00		
09:30		
10:00		
10:30		
11:00		
11:30		
12:00		
12:30		
13:00		
13:30		
14:00		
14:30		
15:00		
15:30		
16:00		
16:30		
17:00		
17:30		
18:00		
18:30		
19:00		
19:30		
20:00		
20:30		
21:00		

Date:

Daily I AMs

I AM

I AM

I AM

I AM

I AM

Tasks I have to do today which contribute to my quarter goals

1.
2.
3.
4.
5.
6.

PRIORITY FOLLOW UP CALL/EMAIL

1.
2.
3.
4.
5.
6.

OTHER TASKS / OR TO DELEGATE

1.
2.
3.
4.
5.

What I used to call "Butterflies," is now classified as "anxiety."

Daily Play Book.

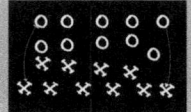

Time	Activity	Outcome / Notes
06:00		
06:30		
07:00		
07:30		
08:00		
08:30		
09:00		
09:30		
10:00		
10:30		
11:00		
11:30		
12:00		
12:30		
13:00		
13:30		
14:00		
14:30		
15:00		
15:30		
16:00		
16:30		
17:00		
17:30		
18:00		
18:30		
19:00		
19:30		
20:00		
20:30		
21:00		

Date:

Daily I AMs

I AM

I AM

I AM

I AM

I AM

Tasks I have to do today which contribute to my quarter goals

1.
2.
3.
4.
5.
6.

PRIORITY FOLLOW UP CALL/EMAIL

1.
2.
3.
4.
5.
6.

OTHER TASKS / OR TO DELEGATE

1.
2.
3.
4.
5.

When your aligned with your purpose, everything begins to come together.

Daily Play Book.

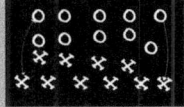

Date:

Time	Activity	Outcome / Notes
06:00		
06:30		
07:00		
07:30		
08:00		
08:30		
09:00		
09:30		
10:00		
10:30		
11:00		
11:30		
12:00		
12:30		
13:00		
13:30		
14:00		
14:30		
15:00		
15:30		
16:00		
16:30		
17:00		
17:30		
18:00		
18:30		
19:00		
19:30		
20:00		
20:30		
21:00		

Daily I AMs

I AM

I AM

I AM

I AM

I AM

Tasks I have to do today which contribute to my quarter goals

1.
2.
3.
4.
5.
6.

PRIORITY FOLLOW UP CALL/EMAIL

1.
2.
3.
4.
5.
6.

OTHER TASKS / OR TO DELEGATE

1.
2.
3.
4.
5.

I remember waiting on a miracle while I was consciously in sin.
How crazy!

Daily Play Book.

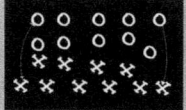

Time	Activity	Outcome / Notes
06:00		
06:30		
07:00		
07:30		
08:00		
08:30		
09:00		
09:30		
10:00		
10:30		
11:00		
11:30		
12:00		
12:30		
13:00		
13:30		
14:00		
14:30		
15:00		
15:30		
16:00		
16:30		
17:00		
17:30		
18:00		
18:30		
19:00		
19:30		
20:00		
20:30		
21:00		

Date:

Daily I AMs

I AM

I AM

I AM

I AM

I AM

Tasks I have to do today which contribute to my quarter goals

1.
2.
3.
4.
5.
6.

PRIORITY FOLLOW UP CALL/EMAIL

1.
2.
3.
4.
5.
6.

OTHER TASKS / OR TO DELEGATE

1.
2.
3.
4.
5.

Miracles come at a price. Be willing to deserve what you pray for. AMEN!

Daily Play Book.

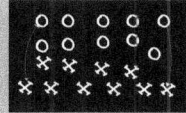

Time	Activity	Outcome / Notes
06:00		
06:30		
07:00		
07:30		
08:00		
08:30		
09:00		
09:30		
10:00		
10:30		
11:00		
11:30		
12:00		
12:30		
13:00		
13:30		
14:00		
14:30		
15:00		
15:30		
16:00		
16:30		
17:00		
17:30		
18:00		
18:30		
19:00		
19:30		
20:00		
20:30		
21:00		

Date:

Daily I AMs

I AM
I AM
I AM
I AM
I AM

Tasks I have to do today which contribute to my quarter goals

1.
2.
3.
4.
5.
6.

PRIORITY FOLLOW UP CALL/EMAIL

1.
2.
3.
4.
5.
6.

OTHER TASKS / OR TO DELEGATE

1.
2.
3.
4.
5.

I had to let go of some very important people for my peace and happiness. Clinking glasses

Daily Play Book.

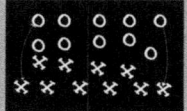

Time	Activity	Outcome / Notes
06:00		
06:30		
07:00		
07:30		
08:00		
08:30		
09:00		
09:30		
10:00		
10:30		
11:00		
11:30		
12:00		
12:30		
13:00		
13:30		
14:00		
14:30		
15:00		
15:30		
16:00		
16:30		
17:00		
17:30		
18:00		
18:30		
19:00		
19:30		
20:00		
20:30		
21:00		

Date:

Daily I AMs

I AM

I AM

I AM

I AM

I AM

Tasks I have to do today which contribute to my quarter goals

1.
2.
3.
4.
5.
6.

PRIORITY FOLLOW UP CALL/EMAIL

1.
2.
3.
4.
5.
6.

OTHER TASKS / OR TO DELEGATE

1.
2.
3.
4.
5.

God perfectly orchestrates moments in life that are worthy to be captured.

Daily Play Book.

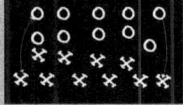

Time	Activity	Outcome / Notes
06:00		
06:30		
07:00		
07:30		
08:00		
08:30		
09:00		
09:30		
10:00		
10:30		
11:00		
11:30		
12:00		
12:30		
13:00		
13:30		
14:00		
14:30		
15:00		
15:30		
16:00		
16:30		
17:00		
17:30		
18:00		
18:30		
19:00		
19:30		
20:00		
20:30		
21:00		

Date:

Daily I AMs

I AM

I AM

I AM

I AM

I AM

Tasks I have to do today which contribute to my quarter goals

1.
2.
3.
4.
5.
6.

PRIORITY FOLLOW UP CALL/EMAIL

1.
2.
3.
4.
5.
6.

OTHER TASKS / OR TO DELEGATE

1.
2.
3.
4.
5.

I stand for empowering others to achieve their greatest potential.

Daily Play Book.

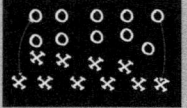

Date:

Time	Activity	Outcome / Notes
06:00		
06:30		
07:00		
07:30		
08:00		
08:30		
09:00		
09:30		
10:00		
10:30		
11:00		
11:30		
12:00		
12:30		
13:00		
13:30		
14:00		
14:30		
15:00		
15:30		
16:00		
16:30		
17:00		
17:30		
18:00		
18:30		
19:00		
19:30		
20:00		
20:30		
21:00		

Daily I AMs

I AM

I AM

I AM

I AM

I AM

Tasks I have to do today which contribute to my quarter goals

1.
2.
3.
4.
5.
6.

PRIORITY FOLLOW UP CALL/EMAIL

1.
2.
3.
4.
5.
6.

OTHER TASKS / OR TO DELEGATE

1.
2.
3.
4.
5.

Bad decisions can ruin your life.

Weekly Summary

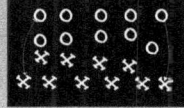

WEEKLY SUMMARY SCORING	Score 1 -10
My focus on TOP weekly priorities...	
My Self Management Time Discipline	
Level of Activity	
Time on Goals	
Self Development	
Health	

BEST PART OF THE WEEK/WHERE WAS OUTSTANDING & HOW I CELEBRATED
•
•
•

TOP LEARNINGS THIS WEEK
•
•
•

TOP CHALLENGES
•
•
•

TOP FOCUS FOR NEXT WEEK
•
•
•

I AM GRATEFUL FOR
•
•
•

PlayBook Calender

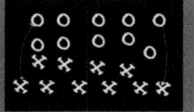

Month:_____   Year:_____

Monday	Tuesday	Wednesday	Thursday	Friday	Saturday	Sunday

Events	Important Dates	Social Events	Meetings

Weekly Playbook Focus Sheet

Name:_____

Weekending:_____   Date:_____ /_____ /_____

*The Number 1 Thing I Must Achieve This Week: _____

*Goals & Actions before next week:	Goal Achieved?	Comments:
Goal 1	☐Yes ☐No	
Goal 2	☐Yes ☐No	
Goal 3	☐Yes ☐No	
Goal 4	☐Yes ☐No	

My brightest achievement in the week just past

My main challenge during the week gone:

Something that I learned through reading, listening to a tape, watching a video or living life:

At the moment, my greatest focus in life is:

I can find help by :

Briefly speaking :   I've concentrated on: I've also worked on:

☐ I spent _____ hrs.   ☐ Health   ☐ Relationships
working ON myself this last
week   ☐ Education   ☐ Communication

☐ My motivation level is at   ☐ Income   ☐ Planning
_____ %
                                   ☐ Love   ☐ Leadership
☐ Life is _____
                                   ☐ Spirituality   ☐ Best Effort

Daily Play Book.

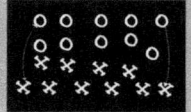

Time	Activity	Outcome / Notes
06:00		
06:30		
07:00		
07:30		
08:00		
08:30		
09:00		
09:30		
10:00		
10:30		
11:00		
11:30		
12:00		
12:30		
13:00		
13:30		
14:00		
14:30		
15:00		
15:30		
16:00		
16:30		
17:00		
17:30		
18:00		
18:30		
19:00		
19:30		
20:00		
20:30		
21:00		

Date:

Daily I AMs

I AM
I AM
I AM
I AM
I AM

Tasks I have to do today which contribute to my quarter goals

1.
2.
3.
4.
5.
6.

PRIORITY FOLLOW UP CALL/EMAIL

1.
2.
3.
4.
5.
6.

OTHER TASKS / OR TO DELEGATE

1.
2.
3.
4.
5.

Choose wisely.

Daily Play Book.

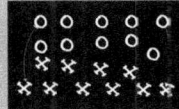

Date: _____

Time	Activity	Outcome / Notes
06:00		
06:30		
07:00		
07:30		
08:00		
08:30		
09:00		
09:30		
10:00		
10:30		
11:00		
11:30		
12:00		
12:30		
13:00		
13:30		
14:00		
14:30		
15:00		
15:30		
16:00		
16:30		
17:00		
17:30		
18:00		
18:30		
19:00		
19:30		
20:00		
20:30		
21:00		

Daily I AMs

I AM

I AM

I AM

I AM

I AM

Tasks I have to do today which contribute to my quarter goals

1.
2.
3.
4.
5.
6.

PRIORITY FOLLOW UP CALL/EMAIL

1.
2.
3.
4.
5.
6.

OTHER TASKS / OR TO DELEGATE

1.
2.
3.
4.
5.

Let no one control how you feel.

Daily Play Book.

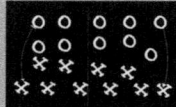

Date:

Time	Activity	Outcome / Notes
06:00		
06:30		
07:00		
07:30		
08:00		
08:30		
09:00		
09:30		
10:00		
10:30		
11:00		
11:30		
12:00		
12:30		
13:00		
13:30		
14:00		
14:30		
15:00		
15:30		
16:00		
16:30		
17:00		
17:30		
18:00		
18:30		
19:00		
19:30		
20:00		
20:30		
21:00		

Daily I AMs

I AM

I AM

I AM

I AM

I AM

Tasks I have to do today which contribute to my quarter goals

1.
2.
3.
4.
5.
6.

PRIORITY FOLLOW UP CALL/EMAIL

1.
2.
3.
4.
5.
6.

OTHER TASKS / OR TO DELEGATE

1.
2.
3.
4.
5.

Today pay attention to the inner dialect of the mind as it attempts to guide you in multiple directions. You just must pay attention and choose the best one.

Daily Play Book.

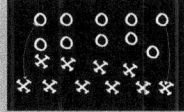

Time	Activity	Outcome / Notes
06:00		
06:30		
07:00		
07:30		
08:00		
08:30		
09:00		
09:30		
10:00		
10:30		
11:00		
11:30		
12:00		
12:30		
13:00		
13:30		
14:00		
14:30		
15:00		
15:30		
16:00		
16:30		
17:00		
17:30		
18:00		
18:30		
19:00		
19:30		
20:00		
20:30		
21:00		

Date:

Daily I AMs
I AM
I AM
I AM
I AM
I AM

Tasks I have to do today which contribute to my quarter goals
1.
2.
3.
4.
5.
6.

PRIORITY FOLLOW UP CALL/EMAIL
1.
2.
3.
4.
5.
6.

OTHER TASKS / OR TO DELEGATE
1.
2.
3.
4.
5.

All things are working for our good. Even when things are not going as we like them to, the problem is a task that exist to be fixed. We have just been ignoring it.

Daily Play Book.

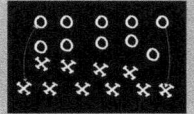

Time	Activity	Outcome / Notes
06:00		
06:30		
07:00		
07:30		
08:00		
08:30		
09:00		
09:30		
10:00		
10:30		
11:00		
11:30		
12:00		
12:30		
13:00		
13:30		
14:00		
14:30		
15:00		
15:30		
16:00		
16:30		
17:00		
17:30		
18:00		
18:30		
19:00		
19:30		
20:00		
20:30		
21:00		

Date:

Daily I AMs

I AM

I AM

I AM

I AM

I AM

Tasks I have to do today which contribute to my quarter goals

1.
2.
3.
4.
5.
6.

PRIORITY FOLLOW UP CALL/EMAIL

1.
2.
3.
4.
5.
6.

OTHER TASKS / OR TO DELEGATE

1.
2.
3.
4.
5.

The question of the day: Who supports you on achieving dreams?

Daily Play Book.

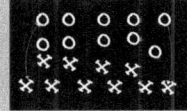

Time	Activity	Outcome / Notes
06:00		
06:30		
07:00		
07:30		
08:00		
08:30		
09:00		
09:30		
10:00		
10:30		
11:00		
11:30		
12:00		
12:30		
13:00		
13:30		
14:00		
14:30		
15:00		
15:30		
16:00		
16:30		
17:00		
17:30		
18:00		
18:30		
19:00		
19:30		
20:00		
20:30		
21:00		

Date:

Daily I AMs

I AM

I AM

I AM

I AM

I AM

Tasks I have to do today which contribute to my quarter goals

1.
2.
3.
4.
5.
6.

PRIORITY FOLLOW UP CALL/EMAIL

1.
2.
3.
4.
5.
6.

OTHER TASKS / OR TO DELEGATE

1.
2.
3.
4.
5.

When chasing your passion, the universe will place exactly what you need to see and experience to get you there. #wiseup

Daily Play Book.

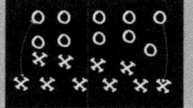

Time	Activity	Outcome / Notes
06:00		
06:30		
07:00		
07:30		
08:00		
08:30		
09:00		
09:30		
10:00		
10:30		
11:00		
11:30		
12:00		
12:30		
13:00		
13:30		
14:00		
14:30		
15:00		
15:30		
16:00		
16:30		
17:00		
17:30		
18:00		
18:30		
19:00		
19:30		
20:00		
20:30		
21:00		

Date:

Daily I AMs

I AM

I AM

I AM

I AM

I AM

Tasks I have to do today which contribute to my quarter goals

1.
2.
3.
4.
5.
6.

PRIORITY FOLLOW UP CALL/EMAIL

1.
2.
3.
4.
5.
6.

OTHER TASKS / OR TO DELEGATE

1.
2.
3.
4.
5.

Focus on the task at hand and not the result. Enjoy this moment and do not let the later get all the praise. The fact that you got up, showed up, developed, and made progress, deserves appreciation.

Weekly Summary

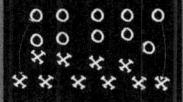

WEEKLY SUMMARY SCORING	Score 1 -10
My focus on TOP weekly priorities...	
My Self Management Time Discipline	
Level of Activity	
Time on Goals	
Self Development	
Health	

BEST PART OF THE WEEK/WHERE I WAS OUTSTANDING & HOW I CELEBRATED
-
-
-

TOP LEARNINGS THIS WEEK
-
-
-

TOP CHALLENGES
-
-
-

TOP FOCUS FOR NEXT WEEK
-
-
-

I AM GRATEFUL FOR
-
-
-

Weekly Playbook Focus Sheet

Name:_____

Weekending:_____   Date:_____ /_____ /_____

*The Number 1 Thing I Must Achieve This Week: _____

*Goals & Actions before next week:	Goal Achieved?	Comments:
Goal 1	☐ Yes ☐ No	
Goal 2	☐ Yes ☐ No	
Goal 3	☐ Yes ☐ No	
Goal 4	☐ Yes ☐ No	

My brightest achievement in the week just past:

My main challenge during the week gone:

Something that I learned through reading, listening to a tape, watching a video or living life:

At the moment, my greatest focus in life is:

I can find help by :

Briefly speaking :   I've concentrated on: I've also worked on:

☐ I spent _____ hrs.   ☐ Health   ☐ Relationships
  working ON myself this last
  week   ☐ Education   ☐ Communication

☐ My motivation level is at   ☐ Income   ☐ Planning
  _____ %
                                      ☐ Love   ☐ Leadership
☐ Life is _____
                                      ☐ Spirituality   ☐ Best Effort

Daily Play Book.

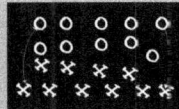

Date:

Time	Activity	Outcome / Notes
06:00		
06:30		
07:00		
07:30		
08:00		
08:30		
09:00		
09:30		
10:00		
10:30		
11:00		
11:30		
12:00		
12:30		
13:00		
13:30		
14:00		
14:30		
15:00		
15:30		
16:00		
16:30		
17:00		
17:30		
18:00		
18:30		
19:00		
19:30		
20:00		
20:30		
21:00		

Daily I AMs

I AM

I AM

I AM

I AM

I AM

Tasks I have to do today which contribute to my quarter goals

1.
2.
3.
4.
5.
6.

PRIORITY FOLLOW UP CALL/EMAIL

1.
2.
3.
4.
5.
6.

OTHER TASKS / OR TO DELEGATE

1.
2.
3.
4.
5.

Kiss the babies, speak life, and tell them you love them this AM. That alone creates a feeling of worth and value. With intention of motivation.

Daily Play Book.

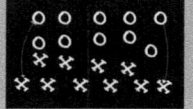

Time	Activity	Outcome / Notes
06:00		
06:30		
07:00		
07:30		
08:00		
08:30		
09:00		
09:30		
10:00		
10:30		
11:00		
11:30		
12:00		
12:30		
13:00		
13:30		
14:00		
14:30		
15:00		
15:30		
16:00		
16:30		
17:00		
17:30		
18:00		
18:30		
19:00		
19:30		
20:00		
20:30		
21:00		

Date:

Daily I AMs

I AM

I AM

I AM

I AM

I AM

Tasks I have to do today which contribute to my quarter goals

1.
2.
3.
4.
5.
6.

PRIORITY FOLLOW UP CALL/EMAIL

1.
2.
3.
4.
5.
6.

OTHER TASKS / OR TO DELEGATE

1.
2.
3.
4.
5.

You be blessed as well!

Daily Play Book.

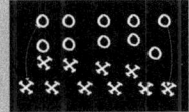

Time	Activity	Outcome / Notes
06:00		
06:30		
07:00		
07:30		
08:00		
08:30		
09:00		
09:30		
10:00		
10:30		
11:00		
11:30		
12:00		
12:30		
13:00		
13:30		
14:00		
14:30		
15:00		
15:30		
16:00		
16:30		
17:00		
17:30		
18:00		
18:30		
19:00		
19:30		
20:00		
20:30		
21:00		

Date:

Daily I AMs

I AM
I AM
I AM
I AM
I AM

Tasks I have to do today which contribute to my quarter goals

1.
2.
3.
4.
5.
6.

PRIORITY FOLLOW UP CALL/EMAIL

1.
2.
3.
4.
5.
6.

OTHER TASKS / OR TO DELEGATE

1.
2.
3.
4.
5.

I have learned that strangers will support you more than family and friends, but I have a few family and friends that will never let me down. Thank you to those who have been down since rock bottom.

Daily Play Book.

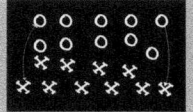

Time	Activity	Outcome / Notes
06:00		
06:30		
07:00		
07:30		
08:00		
08:30		
09:00		
09:30		
10:00		
10:30		
11:00		
11:30		
12:00		
12:30		
13:00		
13:30		
14:00		
14:30		
15:00		
15:30		
16:00		
16:30		
17:00		
17:30		
18:00		
18:30		
19:00		
19:30		
20:00		
20:30		
21:00		

Date:

Daily I AMs

I AM

I AM

I AM

I AM

I AM

Tasks I have to do today which contribute to my quarter goals

1.
2.
3.
4.
5.
6.

PRIORITY FOLLOW UP CALL/EMAIL

1.
2.
3.
4.
5.
6.

OTHER TASKS / OR TO DELEGATE

1.
2.
3.
4.
5.

I wake up in early hours so I can be 100% selfish and take care of ME first.

Daily Play Book.

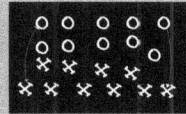

Date:

Time	Activity	Outcome / Notes
06:00		
06:30		
07:00		
07:30		
08:00		
08:30		
09:00		
09:30		
10:00		
10:30		
11:00		
11:30		
12:00		
12:30		
13:00		
13:30		
14:00		
14:30		
15:00		
15:30		
16:00		
16:30		
17:00		
17:30		
18:00		
18:30		
19:00		
19:30		
20:00		
20:30		
21:00		

Daily I AMs

I AM

I AM

I AM

I AM

I AM

Tasks I have to do today which contribute to my quarter goals

1.
2.
3.
4.
5.
6.

PRIORITY FOLLOW UP CALL/EMAIL

1.
2.
3.
4.
5.
6.

OTHER TASKS / OR TO DELEGATE

1.
2.
3.
4.
5.

No matter how much they throw shade. Do not let them stop your shine.

Daily Play Book.

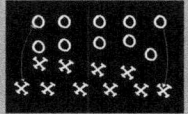

Time	Activity	Outcome / Notes
06:00		
06:30		
07:00		
07:30		
08:00		
08:30		
09:00		
09:30		
10:00		
10:30		
11:00		
11:30		
12:00		
12:30		
13:00		
13:30		
14:00		
14:30		
15:00		
15:30		
16:00		
16:30		
17:00		
17:30		
18:00		
18:30		
19:00		
19:30		
20:00		
20:30		
21:00		

Date:

Daily I AMs

I AM

I AM

I AM

I AM

I AM

Tasks I have to do today which contribute to my quarter goals

1.
2.
3.
4.
5.
6.

PRIORITY FOLLOW UP CALL/EMAIL

1.
2.
3.
4.
5.
6.

OTHER TASKS / OR TO DELEGATE

1.
2.
3.
4.
5.

You know your blessed when you do more with less.

Daily Play Book.

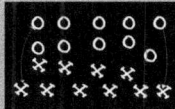

Time	Activity	Outcome / Notes
06:00		
06:30		
07:00		
07:30		
08:00		
08:30		
09:00		
09:30		
10:00		
10:30		
11:00		
11:30		
12:00		
12:30		
13:00		
13:30		
14:00		
14:30		
15:00		
15:30		
16:00		
16:30		
17:00		
17:30		
18:00		
18:30		
19:00		
19:30		
20:00		
20:30		
21:00		

Date:

Daily I AMs

I AM

I AM

I AM

I AM

I AM

Tasks I have to do today which contribute to my quarter goals

1.
2.
3.
4.
5.
6.

PRIORITY FOLLOW UP CALL/EMAIL

1.
2.
3.
4.
5.
6.

OTHER TASKS / OR TO DELEGATE

1.
2.
3.
4.
5.

Once a person feels pain or shame. They will do everything possible to never repeat the feeling.

Weekly Summary

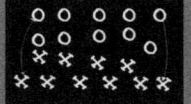

WEEKLY SUMMARY SCORING	Score 1 -10
My focus on TOP weekly priorities...	
My Self Management Time Discipline	
Level of Activity	
Time on Goals	
Self Development	
Health	

BEST PART OF THE WEEK/WHERE I WAS OUTSTANDING & HOW I CELEBRATED
-
-
-

TOP LEARNINGS THIS WEEK
-
-
-

TOP CHALLENGES
-
-
-

TOP FOCUS FOR NEXT WEEK
-
-
-

I AM GRATEFUL FOR
-
-
-

Weekly Playbook Focus Sheet

Name:_____

Weekending:_____   Date:_____ /_____ /_____

*The Number 1 Thing I Must Achieve This Week: _____

*Goals & Actions before next week:		Goal Achieved?	Comments:
Goal 1		☐ Yes ☐ No	
Goal 2		☐ Yes ☐ No	
Goal 3		☐ Yes ☐ No	
Goal 4		☐ Yes ☐ No	

My brightest achievement in the week just past:

My main challenge during the week gone:

Something that I learned through reading, listening to a tape, watching a video or living life:

At the moment, my greatest focus in life is:

I can find help by :

Briefly speaking :

☐ I spent _____ hrs. working ON myself this last week

☐ My motivation level is at _____ %

☐ Life is _____

I've concentrated on:

☐ Health

☐ Education

☐ Income

☐ Love

☐ Spirituality

I've also worked on:

☐ Relationships

☐ Communication

☐ Planning

☐ Leadership

☐ Best Effort

Daily Play Book.

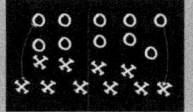

Time	Activity	Outcome / Notes
06:00		
06:30		
07:00		
07:30		
08:00		
08:30		
09:00		
09:30		
10:00		
10:30		
11:00		
11:30		
12:00		
12:30		
13:00		
13:30		
14:00		
14:30		
15:00		
15:30		
16:00		
16:30		
17:00		
17:30		
18:00		
18:30		
19:00		
19:30		
20:00		
20:30		
21:00		

Date:

Daily I AMs

I AM

I AM

I AM

I AM

I AM

Tasks I have to do today which contribute to my quarter goals

1.

2.

3.

4.

5.

6.

PRIORITY FOLLOW UP CALL/EMAIL

1.

2.

3.

4.

5.

6.

OTHER TASKS / OR TO DELEGATE

1.

2.

3.

4.

5.

Before it can be fixed it must be destroyed.

Daily Play Book.

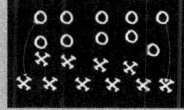

Time	Activity	Outcome / Notes
06:00		
06:30		
07:00		
07:30		
08:00		
08:30		
09:00		
09:30		
10:00		
10:30		
11:00		
11:30		
12:00		
12:30		
13:00		
13:30		
14:00		
14:30		
15:00		
15:30		
16:00		
16:30		
17:00		
17:30		
18:00		
18:30		
19:00		
19:30		
20:00		
20:30		
21:00		

Date:

Daily I AMs

I AM
I AM
I AM
I AM
I AM

Tasks I have to do today which contribute to my quarter goals

1.
2.
3.
4.
5.
6.

PRIORITY FOLLOW UP CALL/EMAIL

1.
2.
3.
4.
5.
6.

OTHER TASKS / OR TO DELEGATE

1.
2.
3.
4.
5.

"God is in control."

Daily Play Book.

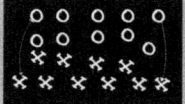

Date:

Time	Activity	Outcome / Notes
06:00		
06:30		
07:00		
07:30		
08:00		
08:30		
09:00		
09:30		
10:00		
10:30		
11:00		
11:30		
12:00		
12:30		
13:00		
13:30		
14:00		
14:30		
15:00		
15:30		
16:00		
16:30		
17:00		
17:30		
18:00		
18:30		
19:00		
19:30		
20:00		
20:30		
21:00		

Daily I AMs

I AM

I AM

I AM

I AM

I AM

Tasks I have to do today which contribute to my quarter goals

1.
2.
3.
4.
5.
6.

PRIORITY FOLLOW UP CALL/EMAIL

1.
2.
3.
4.
5.
6.

OTHER TASKS / OR TO DELEGATE

1.
2.
3.
4.
5.

Even when I am down, I find my way up.

Daily Play Book.

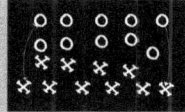

Date:

Time	Activity	Outcome / Notes
06:00		
06:30		
07:00		
07:30		
08:00		
08:30		
09:00		
09:30		
10:00		
10:30		
11:00		
11:30		
12:00		
12:30		
13:00		
13:30		
14:00		
14:30		
15:00		
15:30		
16:00		
16:30		
17:00		
17:30		
18:00		
18:30		
19:00		
19:30		
20:00		
20:30		
21:00		

Daily I AMs

I AM

I AM

I AM

I AM

I AM

Tasks I have to do today which contribute to my quarter goals

1.
2.
3.
4.
5.
6.

PRIORITY FOLLOW UP CALL/EMAIL

1.
2.
3.
4.
5.
6.

OTHER TASKS / OR TO DELEGATE

1.
2.
3.
4.
5.

I had to let go of some very important people for my peace and happiness.

Daily Play Book.

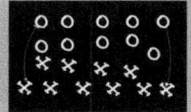

Time	Activity	Outcome / Notes
06:00		
06:30		
07:00		
07:30		
08:00		
08:30		
09:00		
09:30		
10:00		
10:30		
11:00		
11:30		
12:00		
12:30		
13:00		
13:30		
14:00		
14:30		
15:00		
15:30		
16:00		
16:30		
17:00		
17:30		
18:00		
18:30		
19:00		
19:30		
20:00		
20:30		
21:00		

Date:

Daily I AMs

I AM

I AM

I AM

I AM

I AM

Tasks I have to do today which contribute to my quarter goals

1.
2.
3.
4.
5.
6.

PRIORITY FOLLOW UP CALL/EMAIL

1.
2.
3.
4.
5.
6.

OTHER TASKS / OR TO DELEGATE

1.
2.
3.
4.
5.

Say good morning to the first 10 people you encounter this morning. Brighten someone's day.

Daily Play Book.

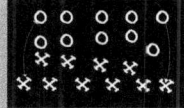

Time	Activity	Outcome / Notes
06:00		
06:30		
07:00		
07:30		
08:00		
08:30		
09:00		
09:30		
10:00		
10:30		
11:00		
11:30		
12:00		
12:30		
13:00		
13:30		
14:00		
14:30		
15:00		
15:30		
16:00		
16:30		
17:00		
17:30		
18:00		
18:30		
19:00		
19:30		
20:00		
20:30		
21:00		

Date:

Daily I AMs

I AM
I AM
I AM
I AM
I AM

Tasks I have to do today which contribute to my quarter goals

1.
2.
3.
4.
5.
6.

PRIORITY FOLLOW UP CALL/EMAIL

1.
2.
3.
4.
5.
6.

OTHER TASKS / OR TO DELEGATE

1.
2.
3.
4.
5.

"No matter how good you are, you can get better."

Daily Play Book.

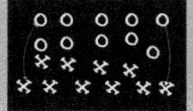

Time	Activity	Outcome / Notes
06:00		
06:30		
07:00		
07:30		
08:00		
08:30		
09:00		
09:30		
10:00		
10:30		
11:00		
11:30		
12:00		
12:30		
13:00		
13:30		
14:00		
14:30		
15:00		
15:30		
16:00		
16:30		
17:00		
17:30		
18:00		
18:30		
19:00		
19:30		
20:00		
20:30		
21:00		

Date:

Daily I AMs

I AM

I AM

I AM

I AM

I AM

Tasks I have to do today which contribute to my quarter goals

1.
2.
3.
4.
5.
6.

PRIORITY FOLLOW UP CALL/EMAIL

1.
2.
3.
4.
5.
6.

OTHER TASKS / OR TO DELEGATE

1.
2.
3.
4.
5.

The way my life is set up, I cannot afford to waste another day.

Weekly Summary

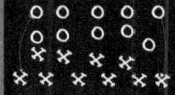

WEEKLY SUMMARY SCORING	Score 1 -10
My focus on TOP weekly priorities…	
My Self Management Time Discipline	
Level of Activity	
Time on Goals	
Self Development	
Health	

BEST PART OF THE WEEK/WHERE I WAS OUTSTANDING & HOW I CELEBRATED
•
•
•

TOP LEARNINGS THIS WEEK
•
•
•

TOP CHALLENGES
•
•
•

TOP FOCUS FOR NEXT WEEK
•
•
•

I AM GRATEFUL FOR
•
•
•

Weekly Playbook Focus Sheet

Name:_____

Weekending:_____   Date:_____ /_____ /_____

*The Number 1 Thing I Must Achieve This Week: _____

*Goals & Actions before next week:	Goal Achieved?	Comments:
Goal 1	☐ Yes ☐ No	
Goal 2	☐ Yes ☐ No	
Goal 3	☐ Yes ☐ No	
Goal 4	☐ Yes ☐ No	

My brightest achievement in the week just past:

My main challenge during the week gone:

Something that I learned through reading, listening to a tape, watching a video or living life:

At the moment, my greatest focus in life is:

I can find help by :

Briefly speaking :

☐ I spent _____ hrs. working ON myself this last week

☐ My motivation level is at _____ %

☐ Life is _____

I've concentrated on:

☐ Health

☐ Education

☐ Income

☐ Love

☐ Spirituality

I've also worked on:

☐ Relationships

☐ Communication

☐ Planning

☐ Leadership

☐ Best Effort

Daily Play Book.

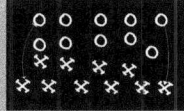

Time	Activity	Outcome / Notes
06:00		
06:30		
07:00		
07:30		
08:00		
08:30		
09:00		
09:30		
10:00		
10:30		
11:00		
11:30		
12:00		
12:30		
13:00		
13:30		
14:00		
14:30		
15:00		
15:30		
16:00		
16:30		
17:00		
17:30		
18:00		
18:30		
19:00		
19:30		
20:00		
20:30		
21:00		

Date:

Daily I AMs

I AM

I AM

I AM

I AM

I AM

Tasks I have to do today which contribute to my quarter goals

1.
2.
3.
4.
5.
6.

PRIORITY FOLLOW UP CALL/EMAIL

1.
2.
3.
4.
5.
6.

OTHER TASKS / OR TO DELEGATE

1.
2.
3.
4.
5.

Today pay attention to the inner dialect of the mind as it attempts to guide you in multiple directions. You just must pay attention and choose the best one.

Daily Play Book.

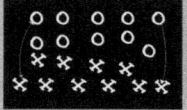

Time	Activity	Outcome / Notes
06:00		
06:30		
07:00		
07:30		
08:00		
08:30		
09:00		
09:30		
10:00		
10:30		
11:00		
11:30		
12:00		
12:30		
13:00		
13:30		
14:00		
14:30		
15:00		
15:30		
16:00		
16:30		
17:00		
17:30		
18:00		
18:30		
19:00		
19:30		
20:00		
20:30		
21:00		

Date:

Daily I AMs

I AM
I AM
I AM
I AM
I AM

Tasks I have to do today which contribute to my quarter goals

1.
2.
3.
4.
5.
6.

PRIORITY FOLLOW UP CALL/EMAIL

1.
2.
3.
4.
5.
6.

OTHER TASKS / OR TO DELEGATE

1.
2.
3.
4.
5.

Sometimes you just must be strong. Its time!

Daily Play Book.

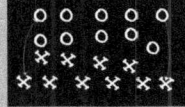

Date:

Time	Activity	Outcome / Notes
06:00		
06:30		
07:00		
07:30		
08:00		
08:30		
09:00		
09:30		
10:00		
10:30		
11:00		
11:30		
12:00		
12:30		
13:00		
13:30		
14:00		
14:30		
15:00		
15:30		
16:00		
16:30		
17:00		
17:30		
18:00		
18:30		
19:00		
19:30		
20:00		
20:30		
21:00		

Daily I AMs

I AM
I AM
I AM
I AM
I AM

Tasks I have to do today which contribute to my quarter goals

1.
2.
3.
4.
5.
6.

PRIORITY FOLLOW UP CALL/EMAIL

1.
2.
3.
4.
5.
6.

OTHER TASKS / OR TO DELEGATE

1.
2.
3.
4.
5.

No matter your belief system, never go a day without prayer.

Daily Play Book.

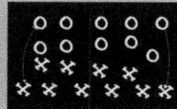

Date:

Time	Activity	Outcome / Notes
06:00		
06:30		
07:00		
07:30		
08:00		
08:30		
09:00		
09:30		
10:00		
10:30		
11:00		
11:30		
12:00		
12:30		
13:00		
13:30		
14:00		
14:30		
15:00		
15:30		
16:00		
16:30		
17:00		
17:30		
18:00		
18:30		
19:00		
19:30		
20:00		
20:30		
21:00		

Daily I AMs

I AM

I AM

I AM

I AM

I AM

Tasks I have to do today which contribute to my quarter goals

1.
2.
3.
4.
5.
6.

PRIORITY FOLLOW UP CALL/EMAIL

1.
2.
3.
4.
5.
6.

OTHER TASKS / OR TO DELEGATE

1.
2.
3.
4.
5.

"Lord why you keep boxing me in, because I'm God's Gift."

Daily Play Book.

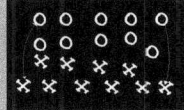

Time	Activity	Outcome / Notes
06:00		
06:30		
07:00		
07:30		
08:00		
08:30		
09:00		
09:30		
10:00		
10:30		
11:00		
11:30		
12:00		
12:30		
13:00		
13:30		
14:00		
14:30		
15:00		
15:30		
16:00		
16:30		
17:00		
17:30		
18:00		
18:30		
19:00		
19:30		
20:00		
20:30		
21:00		

Date:

Daily I AMs

I AM

I AM

I AM

I AM

I AM

Tasks I have to do today which contribute to my quarter goals

1.
2.
3.
4.
5.
6.

PRIORITY FOLLOW UP CALL/EMAIL

1.
2.
3.
4.
5.
6.

OTHER TASKS / OR TO DELEGATE

1.
2.
3.
4.
5.

I am trying to fall in love with myself again. That is my motivation for improvement.

Daily Play Book.

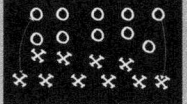

Time	Activity	Outcome / Notes
06:00		
06:30		
07:00		
07:30		
08:00		
08:30		
09:00		
09:30		
10:00		
10:30		
11:00		
11:30		
12:00		
12:30		
13:00		
13:30		
14:00		
14:30		
15:00		
15:30		
16:00		
16:30		
17:00		
17:30		
18:00		
18:30		
19:00		
19:30		
20:00		
20:30		
21:00		

Date:

Daily I AMs

I AM

I AM

I AM

I AM

I AM

Tasks I have to do today which contribute to my quarter goals

1.
2.
3.
4.
5.
6.

PRIORITY FOLLOW UP CALL/EMAIL

1.
2.
3.
4.
5.
6.

OTHER TASKS / OR TO DELEGATE

1.
2.
3.
4.
5.

We must support each other's accomplishments. Stop being jealous and stop hating.

Daily Play Book.

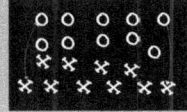

Date:

Time	Activity	Outcome / Notes
06:00		
06:30		
07:00		
07:30		
08:00		
08:30		
09:00		
09:30		
10:00		
10:30		
11:00		
11:30		
12:00		
12:30		
13:00		
13:30		
14:00		
14:30		
15:00		
15:30		
16:00		
16:30		
17:00		
17:30		
18:00		
18:30		
19:00		
19:30		
20:00		
20:30		
21:00		

Daily I AMs

I AM
I AM
I AM
I AM
I AM

Tasks I have to do today which contribute to my quarter goals

1.
2.
3.
4.
5.
6.

PRIORITY FOLLOW UP CALL/EMAIL

1.
2.
3.
4.
5.
6.

OTHER TASKS / OR TO DELEGATE

1.
2.
3.
4.
5.

Take nothing for granted. Especially your life, your love, your joy, and your peace.

Daily Play Book.

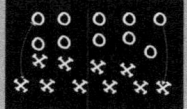

Time	Activity	Outcome / Notes
06:00		
06:30		
07:00		
07:30		
08:00		
08:30		
09:00		
09:30		
10:00		
10:30		
11:00		
11:30		
12:00		
12:30		
13:00		
13:30		
14:00		
14:30		
15:00		
15:30		
16:00		
16:30		
17:00		
17:30		
18:00		
18:30		
19:00		
19:30		
20:00		
20:30		
21:00		

Date:

Daily I AMs

I AM

I AM

I AM

I AM

I AM

Tasks I have to do today which contribute to my quarter goals

1.
2.
3.
4.
5.
6.

PRIORITY FOLLOW UP CALL/EMAIL

1.
2.
3.
4.
5.
6.

OTHER TASKS / OR TO DELEGATE

1.
2.
3.
4.
5.

On this path knowledge is power, but delivery can kill the message. For this reason, development and patience is necessary.

Daily Play Book.

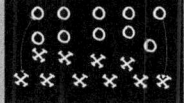

Time	Activity	Outcome / Notes
06:00		
06:30		
07:00		
07:30		
08:00		
08:30		
09:00		
09:30		
10:00		
10:30		
11:00		
11:30		
12:00		
12:30		
13:00		
13:30		
14:00		
14:30		
15:00		
15:30		
16:00		
16:30		
17:00		
17:30		
18:00		
18:30		
19:00		
19:30		
20:00		
20:30		
21:00		

Date:

Daily I AMs

I AM

I AM

I AM

I AM

I AM

Tasks I have to do today which contribute to my quarter goals

1.
2.
3.
4.
5.
6.

PRIORITY FOLLOW UP CALL/EMAIL

1.
2.
3.
4.
5.
6.

OTHER TASKS / OR TO DELEGATE

1.
2.
3.
4.
5.

We all fall guilty of expecting people to treat us better than we treat ourselves.

Weekly Summary

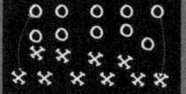

WEEKLY SUMMARY SCORING	Score 1 -10
My focus on TOP weekly priorities...	
My Self Management Time Discipline	
Level of Activity	
Time on Goals	
Self Development	
Health	

BEST PART OF THE WEEK/WHERE I WAS OUTSTANDING & HOW I CELEBRATED
•
•
•

TOP LEARNINGS THIS WEEK
•
•
•

TOP CHALLENGES
•
•
•

TOP FOCUS FOR NEXT WEEK
•
•
•

I AM GRATEFUL FOR
•
•
•

www.ingramcontent.com/pod-product-compliance
Lightning Source LLC
Chambersburg PA
CBHW081426090426
42740CB00017B/3203